71
Arts & Crafts
for
School Children

V&S PUBLISHERS

Published by:

F-2/16, Ansari Road, Daryaganj, New Delhi-110002
☎ 011-23240026, 011-23240027 • *Fax:* 011-23240028
Email: info@vspublishers.com • *Website:* www.vspublishers.com

Branch : Hyderabad
5-1-707/1, Brij Bhawan (Beside Central Bank of India Lane)
Bank Street, Koti, Hyderabad - 500 095
☎ 040-24737290
E-mail: vspublishershyd@gmail.com

Follow us on:

For any assistance sms **VSPUB** to **56161**

All books available at **www.vspublishers.com**

© Copyright: V&S PUBLISHERS
ISBN 978-93-505705-8-6
Edition 2013

The Copyright of this book, as well as all matter contained herein (including illustrations) rests with the Publishers. No person shall copy the name of the book, its title design, matter and illustrations in any form and in any language, totally or partially or in any distorted form. Anybody doing so shall face legal action and will be responsible for damages.

Printed at : Param Offseters, Okhla, New Delhi-110020

Publisher's Note

After the unprecedented success of the books, Drawing & Painting Course I and II (with CDs), both in English and Hindi and a number of similar books, such as 71 + 10 New Science Activities, 71+10 New Science Projects-Junior, etc., V&S Publisers have presently come up with *71 Arts & Crafts for School Children*, a book exclusively designed and written for kids between the age group of 6 to 12 years.

Children love to draw with colours and make crafts, as well. Pencil colours, water and oil colours of different shades, glue, scissors, paper, paints, wax, clay, stones, metal pieces, magnets, leaves, flowers, and many other such easily available materials act as magic tools for them to make their own art and craft creations, with of course, their imaginary skills and elders'(parents or teachers) guidance.

Sometimes, seasons too play a significant role in inducing a child to draw or create something extraordinary, for example: during the long summer holidays of schools which at times could become a little boring for these young ones as even the evenings are too hot to play outdoor games. Similarly, rainy days are also the perfect time to encourage your child's creative instincts by helping them draw or create something interesting. Isn't it?

Our prime motto in publishing this book, or such innovative books is to arouse the creative skills among the kids, particularly the school children by encouraging and teaching them how to draw and make simple craft items with materials that are easily available in and around their surroundings.

However for all these, the help and guidance of teachers/elders/parents is mandatory. So gear up, my dear Young Friends with all your magic tools to create your own Masterpieces!

Contents

Preface 7

Section A : Things to Do With Your Kids 9
- Sculpting 10
- Collage 11
- Marble Painting 12

Section B : Craft Ideas Using Paper, Glue, Tape, Crayons and Markers 13
- Journal 14
- Paper Kite 15
- Greeting Cards 16
- Paper Lantern 17
- Silhouette Cards 18

Section C : Getting Crafty with Paper, Glue and Crayons 19
- Bookmarks 20
- Doorknob Hanger 21
- Paper Necklace 22
- Paper Plate Fish 23
- Paper Sunflower 24
- Make a Balloon Mask 25

Section D : Craft Ideas Using Buttons, Old Socks, or Old Clothes 27
- Button Earrings 28
- Fun Sweatshirt 29
- Sock Puppets 30
- Tank Top Beach Bag 31
- Table Mat 33

Section E : Old Clothes Make the Best Craft Gifts 34
- Blue Jeans Leg Purse 35
- Bead and Button Teacup 36
- Button Bracelets 37
- Button Key Ring 38

Section F : Getting Crafty with Old Clothes-Part Two 39
- Button Flower Brooches 41
- Button Skee-Ball 42

Section G : Craft Ideas Using Food or Kitchen Supplies 43
- Bat Cup 44
- A Bunny Mask 45
- Snowman 46
- Popcorn Tree 47

Section H : Getting Creative with Kitchen Supplies 48
- Flower Pot Hanging 49
- Leprechaun Hat 50
- String Phone 51
- Peanut Puppets 52

Section I : Easy Crafts from Popsicle Sticks 54
- Popsicle Picture Frame 55
- A Pencil Holder 56
- A Butterfly Wand 57
- Sun Mask 58

Section J : Craft Ideas from Nature — 59
- Seashell Wind Chime — 60
- Scented Rocks — 61
- Rock Necklace — 62

Section K : Craft Ideas for the Birds — 63
- Cheerios Bird Feeder — 64
- Bird Binoculars — 65

Section L : Pipe Cleaner Crafts for Kids — 66
- Kids Love Dinosaurs — 67
- Hand Puppets are Fun for Everyone! — 69

Section M : Create Crafts from Nature — 70
- Nature Bracelet — 71
- Switch Plate of Flowers — 72
- Driftwood Door Handle — 73
- Festive Bow and Arrow — 74
- Make a Card of Webbed Veins — 75
- Eco-friendly Holi Colours — 76

Section N : Better than Diamonds: Macaroni Jewellery! — 77
- A Necklace for Every Occasion — 78
- Bracelets Made Easy — 80

Section O : Craft Ideas Using Recycled Materials — 81
- Candleholder — 82
- Soda Can Pen Holder — 83
- Pencil Stand of Bangles — 84
- A Bunny Rabbit — 85
- Can-Do Robots — 86

Section P : Recycle, Reduce and Reuse: Arts and Crafts — 88
- Soda Tab Jewellery — 89
- Bottle Cap Magnets — 90
- Faux Leather Pencil Holder — 91
- Painting Pots — 93
- Coffee Time — 94

Section Q : Go Green with Your Craft Ideas — 95
- Gift Bag Recycling — 96
- Kitty Condo — 97
- Handprint Paper Flowers — 98
- Make Your Own Musical Group — 99
- Paper Sack Costume — 101

Section R : Arts and Crafts for Kids — 103
- Wave Maker — 104
- Treasure Bottle — 105
- Soda Bottle Bird Feeder — 106
- Kazoo — 107

Preface

Crafts and Activities for Kids

Kids love to make crafts. Glue, scissors, paper and paint give them the tools to make creations distinctly on their own. Perfect for rainy days or for encouraging your child's creativity, the crafts and activities we have for your children will bring out their inner artist, architect and designer.

Doing crafts and activities with your child is also the perfect way to spend time with them one on one. Children need their parents participation and attention along with the love and affection in their lives. Hence, making crafts and doing fun activities are a great way to create a lifetime of memories for you and your children.

SECTION A

Things to Do With Your Kids

Coming up with free crafts and activities that you can do with your child will help you to be a part of entertaining them and sparking their creativity. The task may seem difficult to you though, if you have never tried this kind of brainstorming before, or if you are not particularly craft minded. You don't need to feel overwhelmed though. There are many free resources available to you throughout the internet, if you need an idea in a pinch, and in the books that you can get at your local library if you have a bit more time to plan.

Sculpting

Help your children to improve their manual dexterity, engage them in the kitchen, and do some creative art at the same time! Simply take a simple recipe of salted dough, which is made up of flour, salt and water and get started. Your children can help you make the dough and then you can all play with it together. Whether you direct their play by offering up cookie cutters or suggestions of things to make (a person, a chair, a leaf, etc), or you choose to simply let them create things with it, this activity will be a simple hit. The dough's ingredients come from materials which you can easily find in your kitchen and is safe for children to handle. When you are all done with it, i.e., the created small images of animals, birds, flowers, leaves, etc., you can bake the pieces that you and the children have made in the oven and *preserve your artwork for posterity.*

Collage

This activity can be performed like a treasure hunt, either indoors or anywhere outside. If you want to play outside, simply instruct your children to collect leaves, flowers, twigs and other bits of detritus into a bag that you provide. If you'd like to work inside, give them a collection of magazines, glossy advertisements, or even newspaper comics to tear up and cut out shapes and pictures from them. When each child has gathered their material up, provide them with a piece of paper and some basic craft glue. Let them arrange and glue their components to please themselves. When they've finished, you can set the collages they have created to dry before hanging them up or displaying them in some public area. *Wonderful, isn't it?*

Marble Painting

This craft requires you to invest in some water-based paint, if you do not already have it lying around. Alternatively, you could pull some condiments out of the fridge and make this project into an edible art piece. Your other supplies will include a box, a marble or other spherical shaped object, and a piece of paper for each child. Put the paint into easily accessible containers, such as wide jar lids. This allows you to limit the paints your kids have access to and still cover the marble easily. Let your child choose their colour and drop the marble in the box, onto the sheet of paper. Your children can tilt and roll the marble around the box until it runs out of paint or they're ready for a new colour. At the end of the day, they'll have their own *Jackson Pollock style artwork to display*.

SECTION B

Craft Ideas Using Paper, Glue, Tape, Crayons and Markers

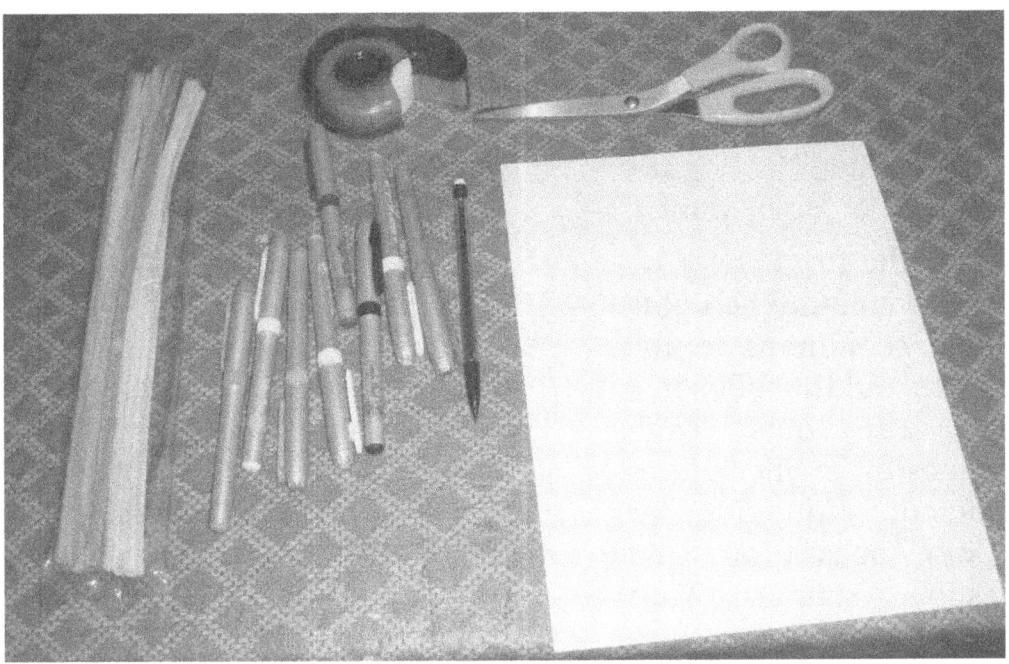

Craft projects for kids are a lot of fun. You can create plenty of things by using simple items, such as paper, some crayons and some glue. Items ranging from hats, to books, greeting cards and bookmarks are just some of the many examples.

Simple craft activities are great ways to show off your child's creativity. Paper is a great product that can be utilised in many different ways. And with all of the available colours provided in crayons and markers, designs can be of anything.

Journal

Why spend money to buy a journal from a book store or any stationery shop? With paper and crayons, a journal created by your own child can be made in no time. All you need is some coloured and white paper, crayons/markers, glue, string and a hole punch.

Create the front cover by choosing a colour. Then glue on some cool items to the cover. This could include some picture cut outs from magazines or smaller pieces of different coloured paper cut into bueautifull and interesting shapes. Your child can even use markers to draw a fascinating design.

Punch three holes in the cover paper and some sheets of white paper. Make sure that all of the holes are aligned properly. Use the string to bind the journal together. It is up to the child to determine how thick or elaborate the journal should be. The pages inside can be either blank pages or lined sheets, but cut them smaller to make a *real paperback book-sized journal*.

Paper Kite

This is a very easy activity. Here are all the items that you may need:
- Legal sized paper
- Plastic straw
- Glue or tape
- String
- Crayons or markers

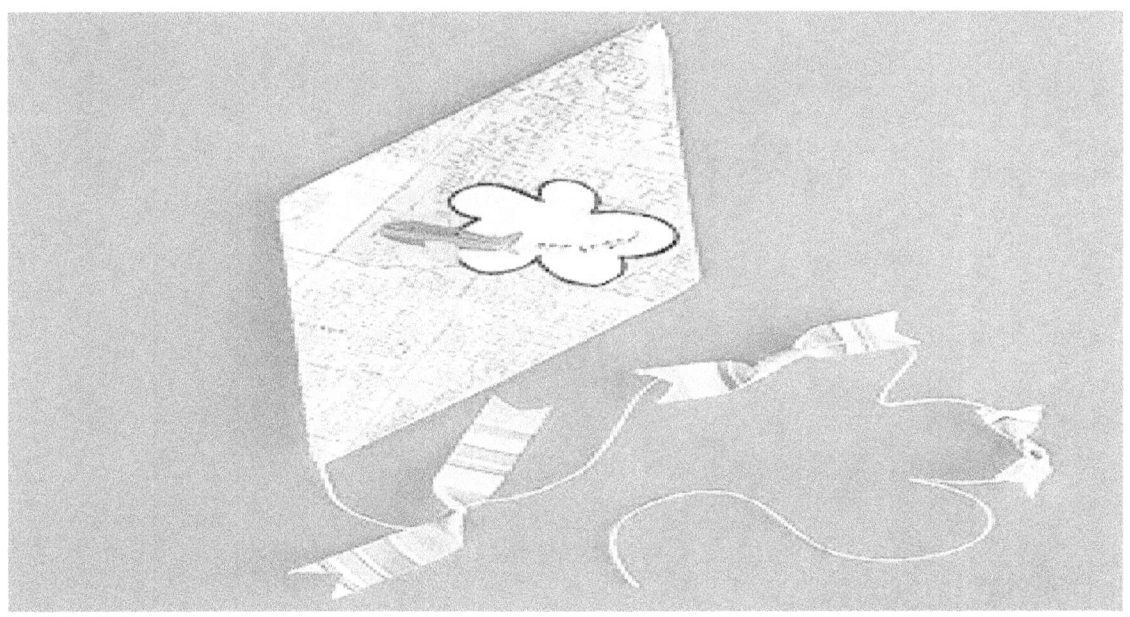

First fold the sheet of a legal sized paper in half. Fold each side at an angle to form a set of wings. Tape or glue the wings together at the fold. Tape a plastic straw across the widest part of the wings to prevent the wings from blowing backwards. Put a small piece of tape to where the string will be put through. Punch a hole in that area and attach the string. The last step is to *colour the kite with crayons or sketch pens or markers to make it bright, attractive and colourful, of course!*.

Greeting Cards

Project 6

For birthdays, anniversaries, holidays or any other special occasion, homemade cards are ideal and the best. All you need is paper and colour pencils or crayons. First take a sheet of paper and fold it in half. The next step is to colour and decorate it as much as your heart desires. Greeting cards can say also much more than words and can be designed in so many different ways. This is a great way for children to express themselves.

Paper Lantern

Here are the materials needed:
- Construction paper
- Scissors
- Glue/tape
- Markers/crayons/sketch pens

Fold the paper into half. Along the folded part, cut evenly spaced slashes on the open side. They should be of about 1-½ inches. Colour with crayons or markers. Open the paper and roll into a tube so that the slashes face downwards. Glue paper edges together. You can hold each end of the lantern and press together to define its shape.

A little tough task to do, yet quite interesting!

Silhouette Cards

Project 8

The things you need:
- ▲ Black chart paper
- ▲ White card sheet
- ▲ Pencil
- ▲ Scissors
- ▲ Glue

Draw an outline of the object on a black chart paper. Cut it along the outline. Make a card from the white card sheet. Now stick the silhouette on top of the card.

Create different kinds of silhouettes with different objects and make new cards each time. Great, isn't it?

SECTION C

Getting Crafty with Paper, Glue and Crayons

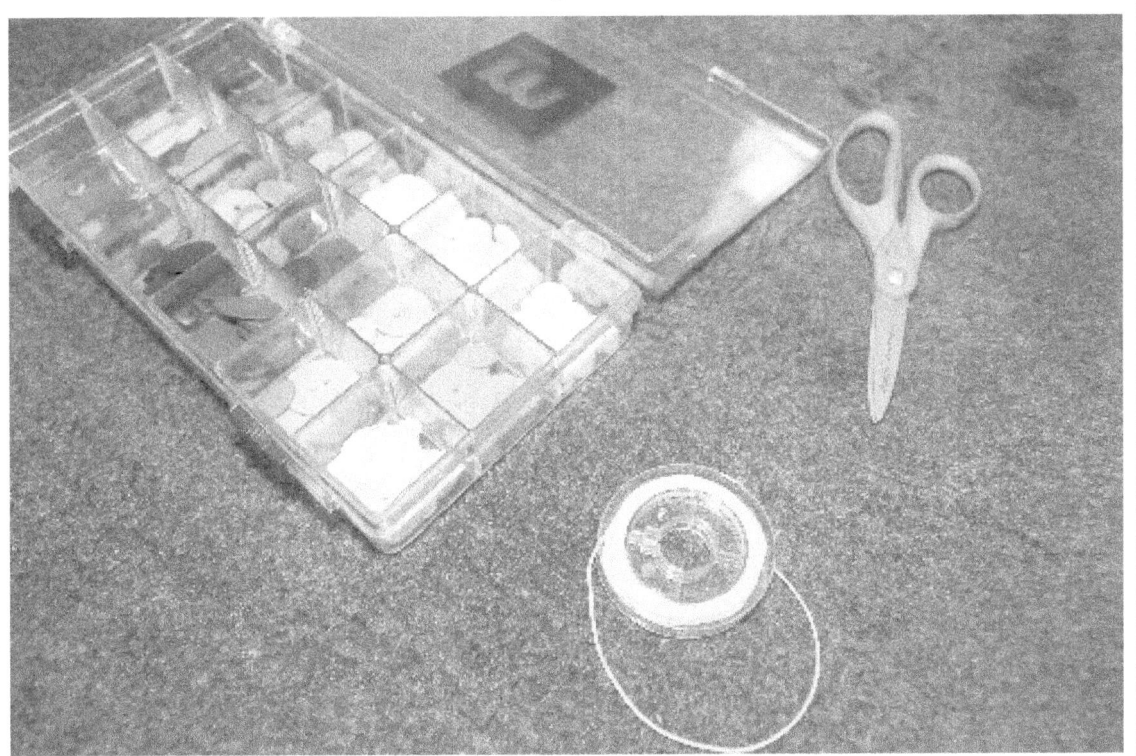

Making art and craft items out of paper is a great fun! Paper can be folded, cut up, or even recycled. Children can really show their creative sides by colouring and drawing unique designs on paper as well.

Here are just a few of the many possibilities for craft ideas, as you proceed further in this book...

Bookmarks

Bookmarks can be designed in so many different ways. Some are large, small, simple or elaborate. Here is what you will need to make your own bookmarks:

- Card stock of any colour
- Markers and/or crayons
- Clear contact paper

The first step is to cut the card stock into the size of your choice. Let your child be free to decorate it as much as he or she wishes to. The last step is to cover the bookmark on each side with a clear contact paper. ***Your colourful bookmark is ready to attract its readers!***

Project 10

Doorknob Hanger

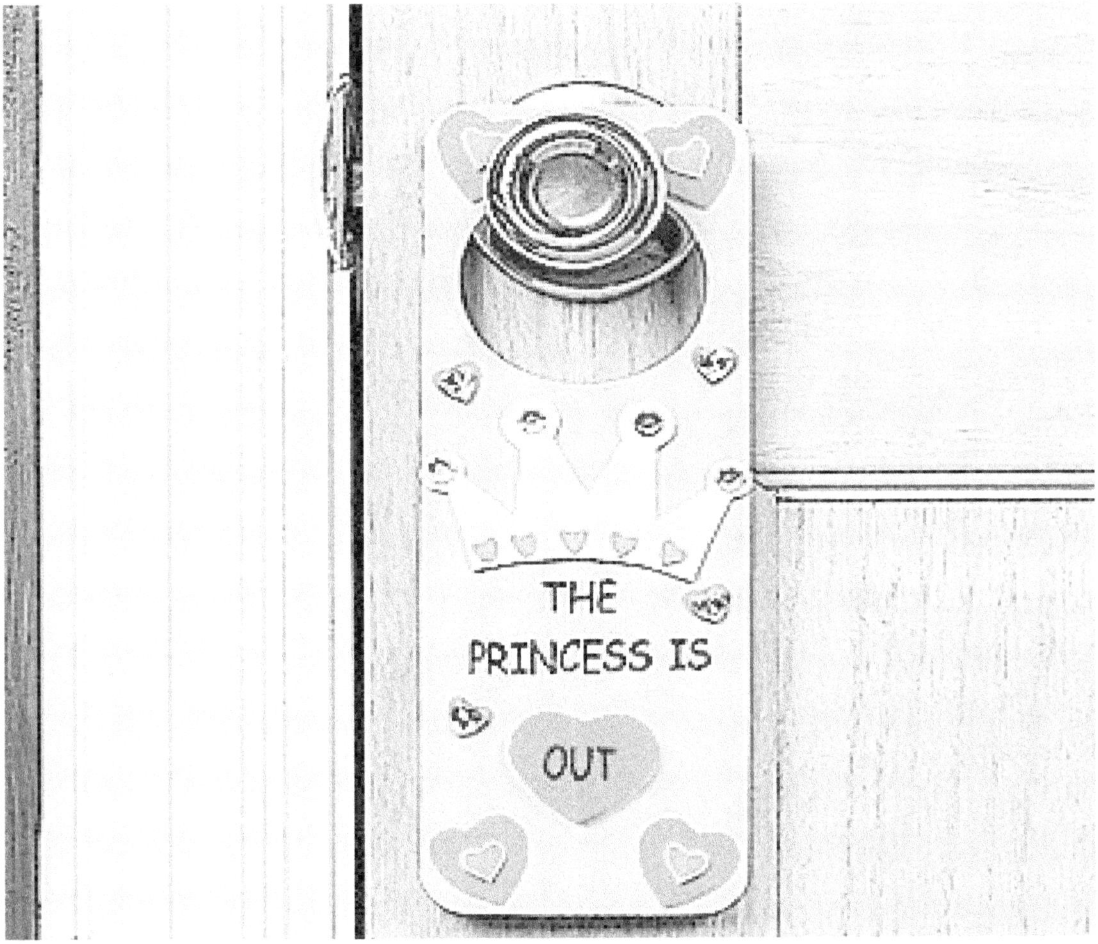

This activity is very simple. All you need is a plain sheet of paper and some markers. Fold a sheet of paper in half and cut at the fold. Hold the half sheet of paper up against a doorknob to estimate its size. Next draw a circle on the paper and have an adult cut it out. Your child can then colour or decorate it as much as he or she wants to. The last step is to hang it on the door! ***looks great! Isn't it?***

Paper Necklace

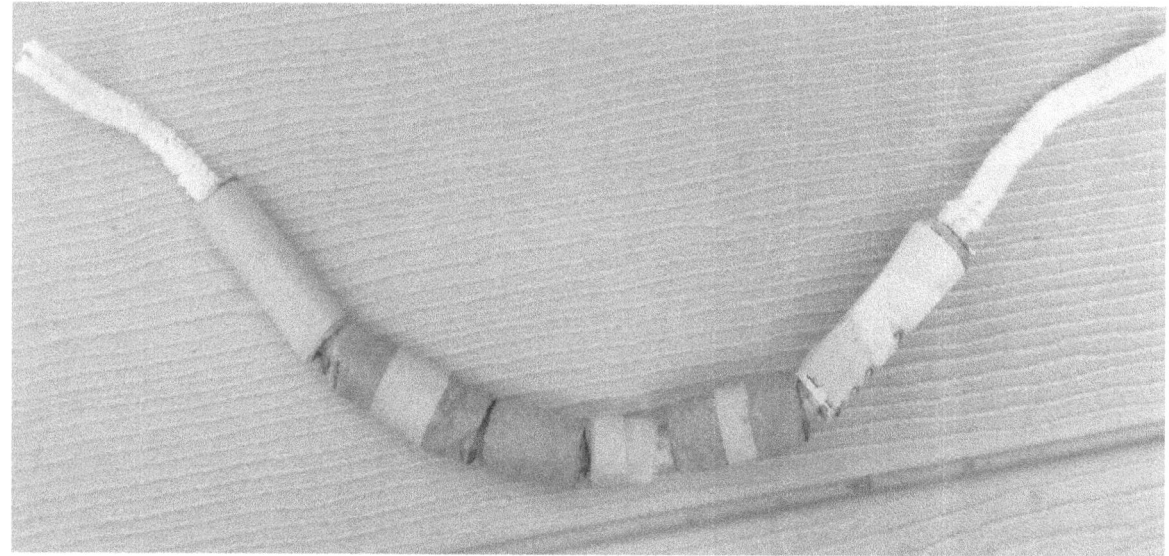

Here are the materials needed:
- Paper
- A pencil
- White glue
- Scissors
- String
- Crayons or markers

First cut the paper into thin rectangular strips. Colour and decorate on the strips. Place some glue on one edge of each strip. Wrap the paper around the pencil with the unglued piece overlapping the glued piece. When the glue is dry, slip the pieces off the pencil. The last step is to lace the string through the pieces of the colourfully decorated strips to create the necklace. ***Gorgeous, isn't it?***

Project 12

Paper Plate Fish

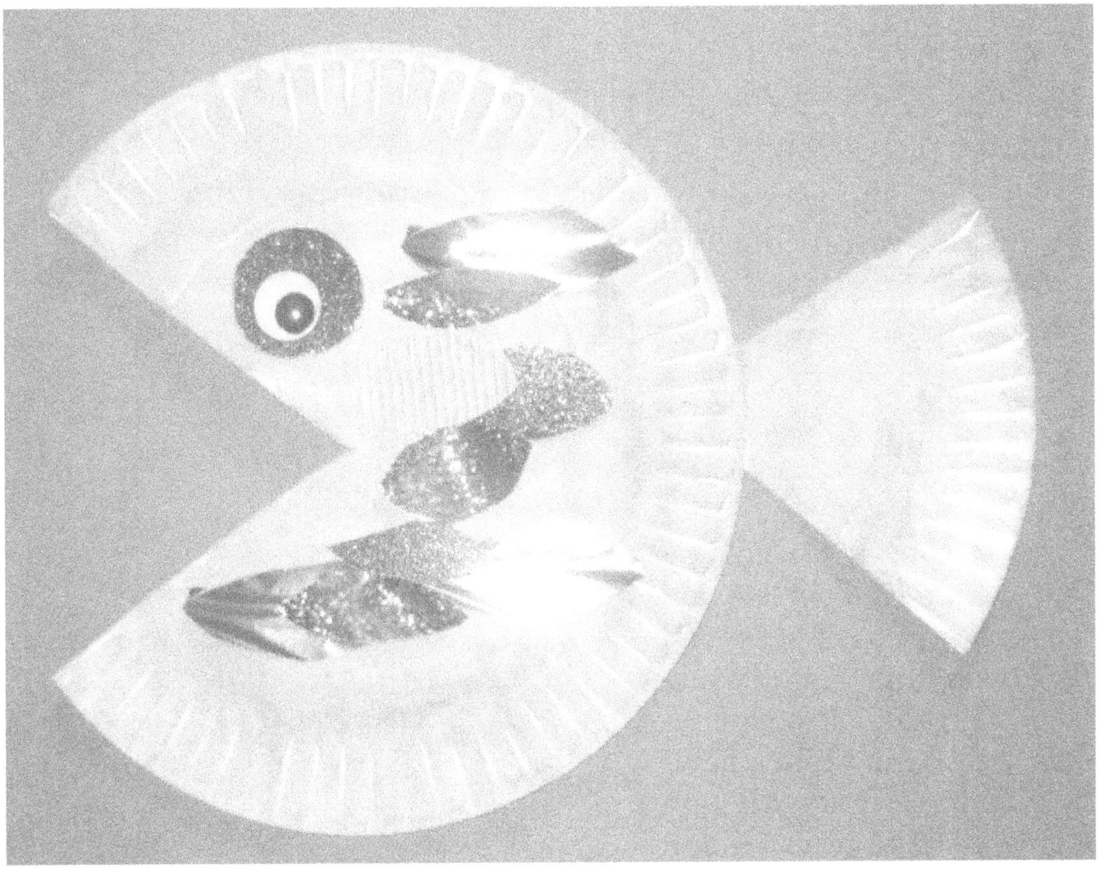

This craft is simple as well as very funny. First cut a wedge out of a paper plate. This edge will serve as your fish's tail. Glue the tail to the end of the paper plate (fish). Draw eyes on the fish using markers, or crayons. To make it even more attractive, add a googly eye instead. Colour the fish with as many colours as you desire by drawing scales or lips. ***Looks like a real fish indeed!***

Paper Sunflower

Project 13

Add some colour to your classroom or home. Here are the materials you will require to make a beautiful and vibrant sunflower:

- Small paper plate
- Paper towel tube
- Green construction paper
- Yellow construction paper
- Scissors
- Pencil
- Tape/glue
- Stapler

First create the stem by wrapping green construction paper around the paper towel tube. Hold it together by using either tape or glue. To create the petals, trace your child's hand onto the yellow construction paper and then cut out. You will need about six of these. Staple the handprints around the paper plate.

The last and the final step is to staple the stem to the paper plate. Flatten one end of the stem to make it easier to staple. You can repeat this activity several times to create a beautiful bouquet!

Make a Balloon Mask

Things you need:
- A big balloon
- Adhesive
- Bowl of water
- Poster colours, sketch pens,
- Paint brushes
- A knife
- Thread
- A screwdriver
- An old newspaper

Blow the balloon and tie it with a string. Then draw a line on it with a sketch pen, dividing the balloon into two equal halves.

Now tear the newspaper into small bits. Dip the torn bits in water and place them on any one side of the balloon.

Stick three layers of wet paper on the balloon, placing them over each other. Spread adhesive evenly on the wet paper. Mix some adhesive in the water and put more paper bits into it. Place several more layers of these bits on the balloon. You should put at least six layers in the second round.

After placing the last layer of wet paper bits on the balloon, smoothen it with your hands to make it an even surface.

Keep the balloon to dry at room temperature. It may take a day or more for the paper to dry completely.

After drying, the size of the balloon will reduce. Remove the balloon. A stiff bowl-like container will come out. Now it is ready to become a mask.

After this, you have to draw a face on the bowl to make the mask. Draw the eyes, nose and mouth with a sketch pen. Give whatever expressions you want to the mask you have created.

With a heated knife, cut out the paper from the area where you have drawn the eyes. This way you can see through the mask, when you wear it.

Make two holes on the mask where the ears should be with a heated screwdriver. Now paint the mask with any colour you desire, using water/ poster colours. Let the paint dry. It will take between half-an-hour to forty-five minutes.

To give a strong and bright coat of paint, mix some adhesive with the colour and then apply on the mask.

You can make the mask as dramatic as you want. Use your imagination. Make the face of the devil or make a doll, a fairy or a clown.

Your mask is complete. All you need to do is to put a string through the holes on either side of the mask and wear it to look funny or scare people around!

SECTION D

Craft Ideas Using Buttons, Old Socks, or Old Clothes

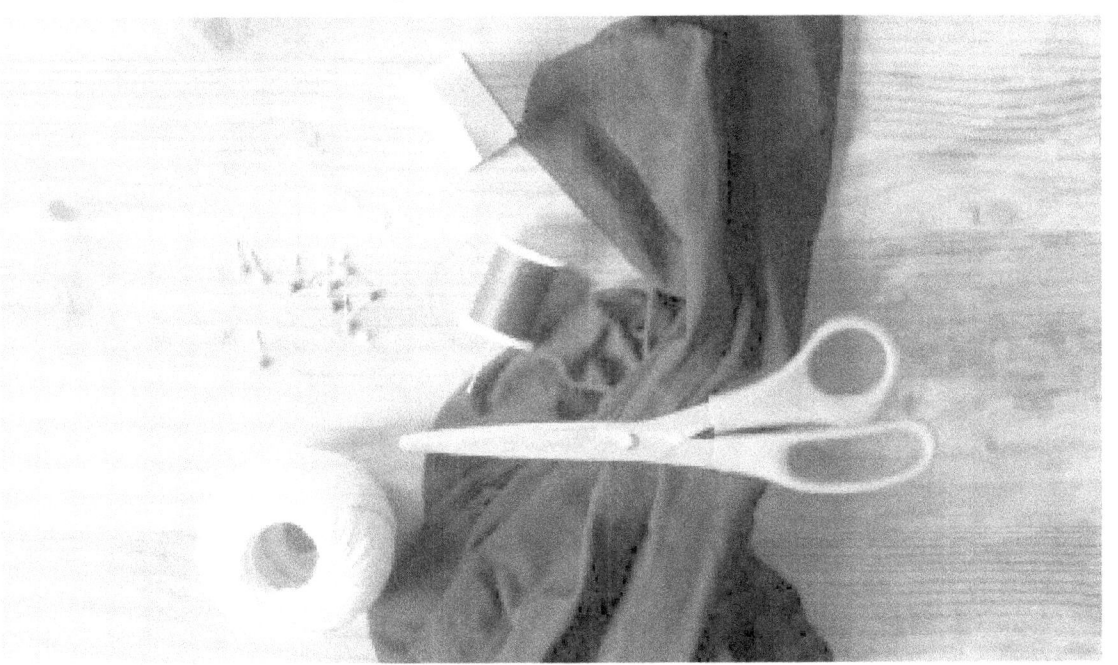

Arts and crafts are fun because they can be created out of so many things. Items found around the house, such as buttons, socks, or clothes can be creatively put together to make something unique and have fun. Children can really show off their artistic skills by getting involved with arts and crafts.

Art and Craft activities always involve a little bit of patience and systematic approach. Instructions need to be followed and the proper materials should all be handy. These activities are great for children because they really encourage them to learn new things, and also learn at the same time, how to pay attention to details and improve one's concentration of mind.

Button Earrings

Project 15

For a cute pair of earrings, here is what you will need:
- A pair of matching buttons
- Jewellery glue
- Flat earring backs

Smoother and flatter buttons work better for this activity. All you need to do is apply glue to the back of the buttons and then place against the earring backs. Your simple, easy and stylish buttons are ready!

Project 16 — Fun Sweatshirt

Got an old sweatshirt that needs a touch of cute style? Apply some buttons! The only other materials that you will need are thread, needles and scissors.

Lay your old sweatshirt flat. Then get your designer skills going by creating a pattern with the buttons. Sew them into different places as per your desire and creative skills. ***Your Designer Sweatshirt is ready!***

Sock Puppets

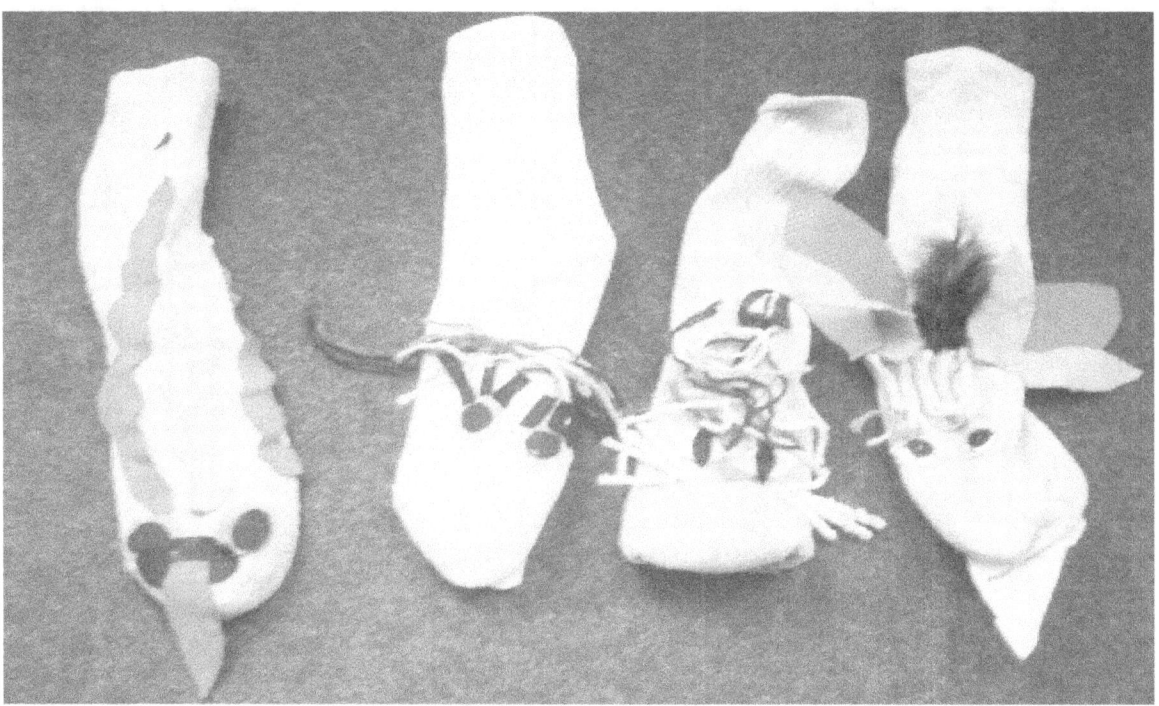

For some reason, we always lose socks in the laundry. The black hole at the bottom of our washers and dryers always seem to win in this battle. What we are left with are random socks that go around solo and therefore, can be useless if it doesn't match with any other lose socks. These socks can be used creatively to prepare *sock puppets*.

Sock puppets are easy and fun! All it takes is a lose sock, a child's arm and some creative decorating. Use a black permanent marker or googly eyes so that your puppet can see. Glue on the cut out pieces of construction paper or felt for the ears. Depending on how much time or how elaborate your child would like to decorate the sock puppets, the many things that you can make with sock puppets are limitless. You can stick or stitch buttons, coloured ribbons, threads, etc.

Project 18
Tank Top Beach Bag

Save one of your child's old tank tops to make a bag for warm days at the beach. Here are the materials that you need:

- ▲ Tank top
- ▲ Some trim
- ▲ One yard of cord
- ▲ Appliqués

- Fabric glue
- Scissors
- Safety pin

Cut open about 1" of the hem of the tank top. Attach a safety pin to the end of the cord and push through the opening into the hem. Work the cord and pin around the bottom until you reach the opening of the hem again. Remove the safety pin once you see both the ends of the cord sticking out.

Using the end of the cord, pull up from the bottom of the tank top and gather until it is as tight as you can get it. Double knot towards the and tie the ends together. Trim the ends and push up the knot inside of the hem. Glue an appliqué to the bottom of the bag. Then decorate your beach bag as much as you wish depending upon the materials you have and your creative skills!

Table Mat

You can make mats of varying sizes and colours and give them as gifts or souvenirs to your family and friends.

The things you need:
- Pieces of old cloth
- Adhesive or glue

Cut the cloth in three strips, half-an-inch wide.

Hold the strips together and tie a knot at the end.

Plait the strips until you get a length of half-a-metre.

Now keeping the knotted end in the centre, wind the plaited strips. Stick the other end to the wound bundle. Your handmade Table Mat is ready for us!

This mat has many utilities, such as: base for telephone and showpieces, wall hangings and you can also use it just about anywhere in the house.

SECTION E

Old Clothes Make the Best Craft Gifts

Old buttons, socks and clothes can be turned into really fun things or craft items. Before throwing these stuff out or donating them to the Needy, see what kinds of crafts you can make with your child. Craft items are great for gift ideas. They can also turn what you once thought was useless into something useful. There are lots of suggestions for these craft items and I bet that your child will be excited to embark on a cool activity.

Blue Jeans Leg Purse

Before throwing your old pair of jeans away, make a smart-looking purse for your daughter or give it as a gift to somebody.

Here is what you need:
- Old jeans
- Needle and thread
- Appliqué
- Scissors

Cut the legs off of a pair of old jeans. Then cut the hem. One leg will be used for the purse and the other for the strap. Sew across the bottom of one of the legs and sew about 1" from the edge. Snip up to the sewing line every " for some frays. Repeat these steps for the top of the purse.

Cut the other leg half into nine " strips. Tie the ends together and braid. Sew to the top of the purse. Stitch on appliqué and decorate as freely as you want. Your purse looks really trendy! Isn't it?

Bead and Button Teacup

This makes a very colourful and pretty gift for an aunt or grandmother. Here are the materials that you will require:

- Solid coloured teacups with saucers
- Decorative beads and buttons
- Hot glue gun
- Glue sticks
- Tweezers

Wash the teacup or teacups to ensure that they are completely clean. Using the hot glue gun, glue the decorative beads and buttons onto the teacup. You can also glue beads and buttons to the outer rim of the saucer as well. To prevent from burning yourself and to give you an easier and convenient time for arranging all the above, use the tweezers.

Note: Tweezers are small pincers or nippers for picking up small ojbects, etc.

Button Bracelets

There is nothing like creating your own jewellery. Your daughter will love making these to wear on her wrist. For little boys, they can use them as *Friendship Bands* or give away these bracelets to their sisters or friends!

What you will need are colourful buttons and elasticised cords. Cut the cord so that it is long enough to wrap around a wrist twice. Thread the cord through the holes of the back of the buttons to the front and then back again. Once that is complete with every button, thread both the ends of the elastic through a metal crimp tube. Using pliers, squeeze it tightly. Then trim the excess elastic with scissors or a knife. *Your exclusive Button Bracelets look really great!*

Button Key Ring

Project 23

Do you always lose your keys somewhere? Why not keep them intact with a new key ring? What you will need are ten buttons and 12 inches of fine cord. First fold the cord in half and make a knot about one inch from the fold. Thread the buttons onto the cord and push each end of the cord through one of the holes in the buttons.

When the last button is threaded, knot the ends of the cord. Cut off the excess cord. Slip the loop of the cord into the key ring.

Wow! Your Key Ring is ready to use.

SECTION F

Getting Crafty with Old Clothes-Part Two

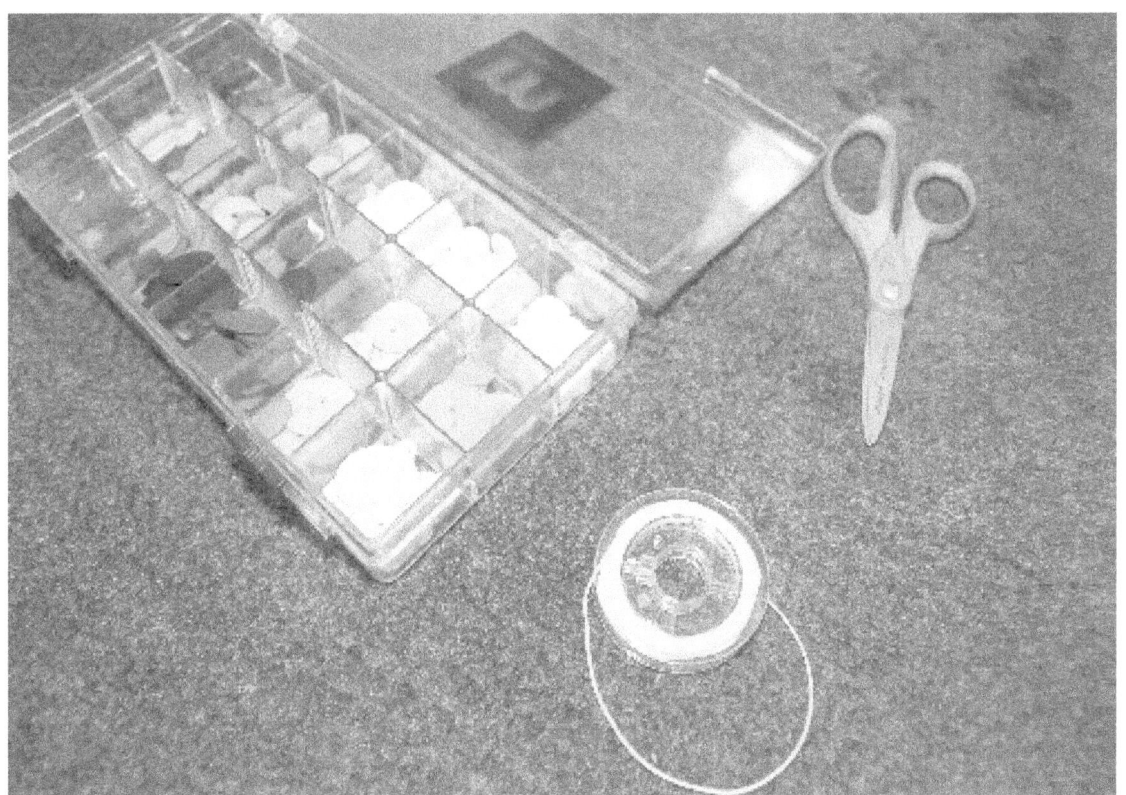

Random items lie around the house with no real use. When things get overused or worn out, they tend to be disposed of or left in a corner of the house somewhere. Reusing old or random things is a great way to not let things go to complete waste. Teaching your child about reusing and recycling things is a great lesson to learn.

Go around your house and collect as many random items as you can find with your child or children, such as, old buttons, torn clothes, plastic bottles, coloured paper pieces, etc. Go through the bedrooms and find some mismatched socks. If your child has outgrown his or her clothes, it would be a great idea to save them for some art and craft before throwing them out or giving them away. Reusing and recycling things teaches children how to conserve and not be wasteful. There are so many different types of materials in the world that can be transformed into something else. Saving items to reuse also means saving the planet.

Once you and your child have collected those random and reusable items, try out some of these wonderful craft activities. Some may be a little harder than others, and some may require a lot of time. Regardless of all these factors, these activities are fun and teach kids the importance of using things wisely and creatively.

The following craft activities are a great fun as well as a creative lesson that you can and must do with your child to enhance his/her own creative mind and skills!

Button Flower Brooches

Brooches or Broaches can add style to any outfit. Here is what you will need:
- Two green pipe cleaners
- Five buttons
- 12 inches of ribbon, wide
- inch pin back
- Scissors
- Ruler
- Needle nose pliers
- Glue gun
- Glue sticks

First cut the pipe cleaners into 4" strips. Slip a stem through the hole in a button going from the back and then to the front. At the back, twist the stem tightly using the needle nose pliers. Gather the pipe cleaners together and wrap them with the last pipe cleaner. Trim the ends.

Bend the flowers to make the bouquet flat. Pull some of the pipe cleaners to create varying lengths. Trim the bottom of the stem and tie a ribbon into a bow at the centre. Glue the pin back to back of your beautiful, button brooch!

Button Skee-Ball

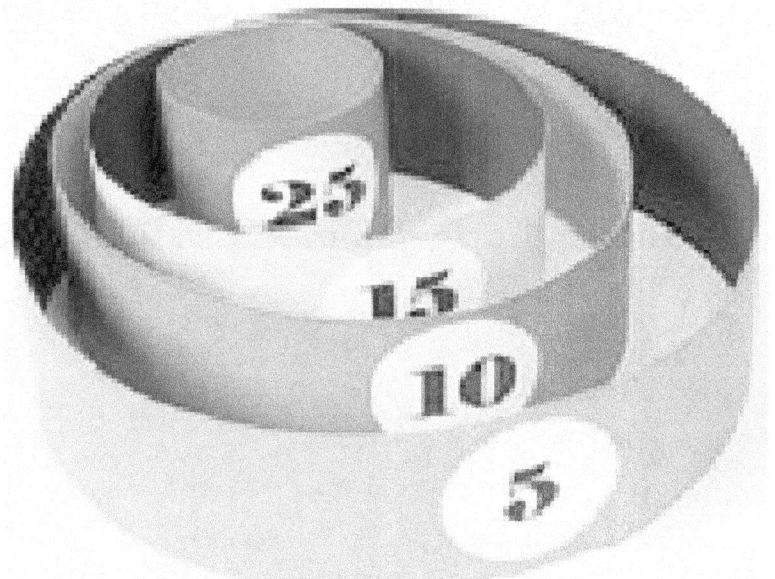

A fun mini version of the game. These are the materials that you'll require:

Two-inch wide poster boards (28, 21, 17 and eight inches long)
- Double sided tape
- Black pen
- Felt
- One large button
- Ten small buttons

First take each poster board and secure the seams with double-sided tape. Write point values on each one with your black pen. Assemble the poster boards into rings as it is in a Skee-Ball with smaller rings inside the larger ones. Cut out a piece of felt and use it as a launch pad. Use the large button to launch the ten smaller buttons. *Have fun, as your amazing Button Skee-Ball is ready to play!*

SECTION G

Craft Ideas Using Food or Kitchen Supplies

Paper plates may seem like ordinary things, but they can actually be transformed into fun, crafty projects. With enough creativity, paper plates can turn into various things. Just add a little colour and a pizzazz and you have got yourself a new decorative piece. With the holidays approaching, the possibilities are endless to create colourful ornaments, wall hangings and gifts!

The following is a list of some fun holiday craft ideas using paper plates!

Bat Cup

For Halloween or Diwali, this batty creation will bring plenty of smiles. Here are the materials that you will need:

- Tin can
- Paper plate
- Black and white paint
- Wiggle eyes
- Glue
- Scissors
- Paintbrush

First start off by painting the tin can and the plate black. Using the white paint, add a mouth. Then glue on the wiggle eyes. Once the paint is dry, cut the paper plate in half. Cut the scalloped edges along the straight sides of the paper plate to create wings. The last and final step is to glue the wings to the can. Enjoy!

A Bunny Mask

Although Easter could be ways away, it is never too early to be prepared once spring comes around again. Making a bunny mask is a lot of fun. Here is what you need:

- Paper plate
- Pink paint
- White pipe cleaner
- Pink card
- Elastic thread
- Glue
- Black pen

The first step is to paint the back of the paper plate with the pink paint. Let it sit to the side until it is completely dry. Once it's dry, cut out two eye holes. Cut the pipe cleaner into three separate pieces and twist together at the centre. Then glue it to the centre of the paper plate (face).

Cut out the bunny's nose from the pink card and glue it onto the pipe cleaners. The pipe cleaners should stick out like whiskers. Cut out two ears from the pink card and glue to the top of the paper plate. Use the black pen to draw the bunny's mouth. Use the butt of the pen to punch two holes on either side of the face. String the elastic thread through for the final step of the mask. *Your cute, little Bunny Mask is ready!*

Snowman

Project 28

For those cold, wintry days, make a little snowman to keep you company. Here is what you need:

- Two paper plates
- Red and black construction paper
- Orange pipe cleaner
- Hole punch
- Crayons
- Scissors
- Glue
- Yarn

Cut off the rim of one of the plates, to make it smaller. Punch a hole near the rim on both plates. Using the yarn, tie the plates together. Draw and cut out a hat and two boots from the black construction paper. Draw and cut out mittens from the red paper. Glue the pieces onto the snowman.

The last steps are to draw the eyes, a mouth and buttons. The orange pipe cleaner can be poked through the top plate for the nose. Wow! Your snowman looks like a real one.

Project 29
Popcorn Tree

If you are tired of eating popcorns, try something new: decorate your room with them. This is how you can do it.

All you need is:
- A thorny stem of a plant or a bush
- Popcorns
- A bowl

Pick up a thorny stem from a plant or a bush - if it has leaves, remove them.

Put a popcorn on the tip of each thorn carefully. Avoid pricking yourself.

Put some mud in a bowl and fix your stem in it.

Use this popcorn arrangement to decorate your room.

You can also paint the popcorns to make them look brighter. Once the popcorns lose their colour or begin to fall, use something else instead. It looks like a Japanese Ikebana! Isn't it?

SECTION H

Getting Creative with Kitchen Supplies

Making crafts out of food supplies is a lot of fun. By using items, such as paper cups, paper napkins, or paper plates, you can turn ordinary products into something cool and colourful. Crafts can be made out of the simplest things, and you don't get much simpler than paper. Homemade crafts show off a child's creativity. It is easy to buy something from the store, but when it is created by a child, it makes it all the more special. Receiving a gift that was made by your child is touching and very much appreciated. Crafts can keep kids busy and enlighten them in so many ways.

In order to give these wonderful creations away and show them off, let's get busy by making these cool items.

Flower Pot Hanging

This is a great gift for moms, aunts, teachers, or grandmothers. The best part is that this lasts forever in comparison to flowers! Here is what you need:

- Large paper plate
- Paper cup
- Paint
- Glue
- String
- Hole punch
- Green tissue paper

First paint the paper plate. Then cut the paper cup in half. Your child can paint the cup too if he or she wishes. Let these items dry for a while and then glue the cup onto the plate. After that is finished drying, punch a hole at the top of the plate and put a string through it. Tie a ribbon to create a loop that would fit over a doorknob.

Cut the green tissue paper into pieces that are 4"x4". Tuck them into the cup to create the illusion of leaves. Or if preferred, you can fold the tissue paper accordion-like to make them look like grass. Interesting, isn't it?

Leprechaun Hat

To prepare for the next St. Patrick's holiday or for fancy dress party, here is an easy activity for a very festive hat. What you will need are a small paper plate, a paper cup, paint, glue and construction paper.

Paint the paper plate and outside of the paper cup green. Put them aside to dry. Once drying is finished, glue the cup upside down in the centre of the plate's bottom. Cut a piece of construction paper that is wide enough and will fit around the paper cup where it is glued to the plate. Glue it to the cup. Cutting out a small yellow buckle from construction paper is a fun option, too.

String Phone

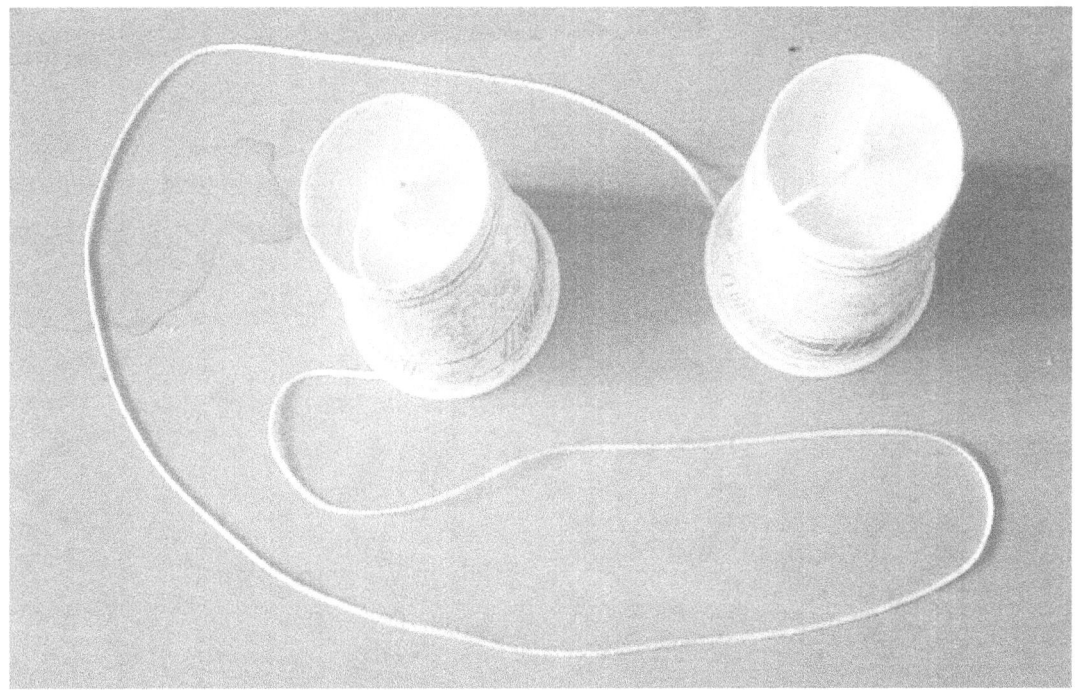

This is a very popular activity and is an every child's favourite. In order to make a string phone, you will need the following supplies:

- ▲ Paper cups (2)
- ▲ A nail
- ▲ Paper clips (2)
- ▲ A piece of string (5-10 feet long)

Using the nail, first poke holes in the bottom of the two cups. Push the string through the hole of one of the cups and tie it to a paper clip in the inside. Repeat this step with the second cup. Now you are ready to chat with your friend as you do in a phone!

Peanut Puppets

You will need:
- A darning needle
- A reel of strong thread
- Peanuts in the shell (at least 13, of different sizes)
- Paint

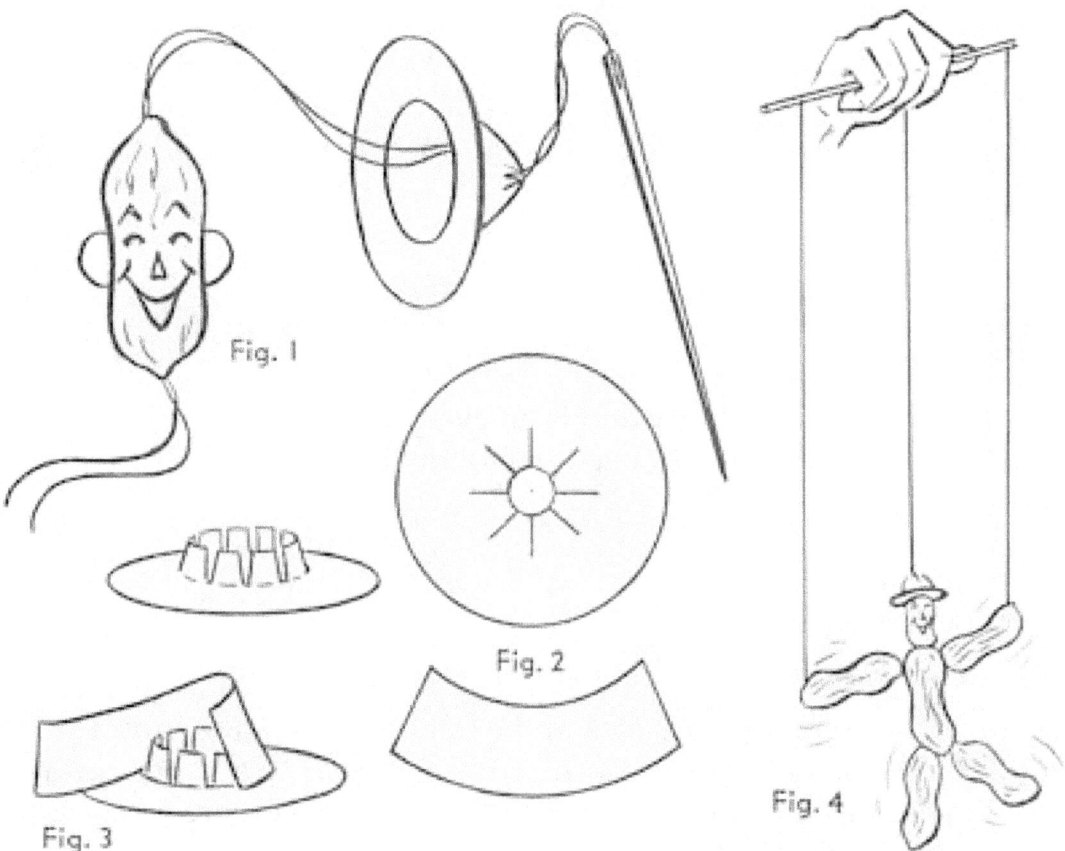

Fig. 1

Fig. 2

Fig. 3

Fig. 4

- Paintbrushes
- Glue
- Scissors
- Wool for hair
- 3 lollipops
- Ice cream sticks or twigs

Procedure: Thread the needle and make a large knot in the end. To make the head and body, thread three long peanuts on to the length of thread. (You may need to twist the needle a bit to get it through the shell). Leave a long thread above the head. To make the hands, arms and legs, string long and small peanuts to the body, as shown.

Remember to tie knots in the thread so that the peanuts won't fall off.

Paint the puppet, and leave it to dry. Glue wool on the head to make hair. Leave the long thread above the head free of hair and glue.

Make the control stick by gluing three sticks together, as shown. Attach the control threads. Tie the hands to the front cross-piece and the feet to the back. Tie the head to the centre control stick. Dab glue on to the control stick where the threads are tied. This will stop the threads from slipping.

You can use your imagination to make paper dresses, hats, etc.

SECTION 1

Easy Crafts from Popsicle Sticks

Popsicle stick crafts are fun and teach children how to be creative. With the right amount of patience, a child along with his or her parent can prepare many different things.

Here are five ways to make Popsicle sticks into something very interesting.

Project 34
Popsicle Picture Frame

This can create a really great gift for Mom or Dad's birthday. The materials needed are 9" x 12" white paper, eight Popsicle sticks, glue, crayons and scissors. Two Popsicle sticks go on each side, and will be glued to the paper in a square shape. This creates the frame. With the crayons, the child can colour the Popsicle sticks, as well as draw pictures on the frame, as shown. After this is done, the excess paper can be cut away from the picture frame.

A Pencil Holder

Project 35

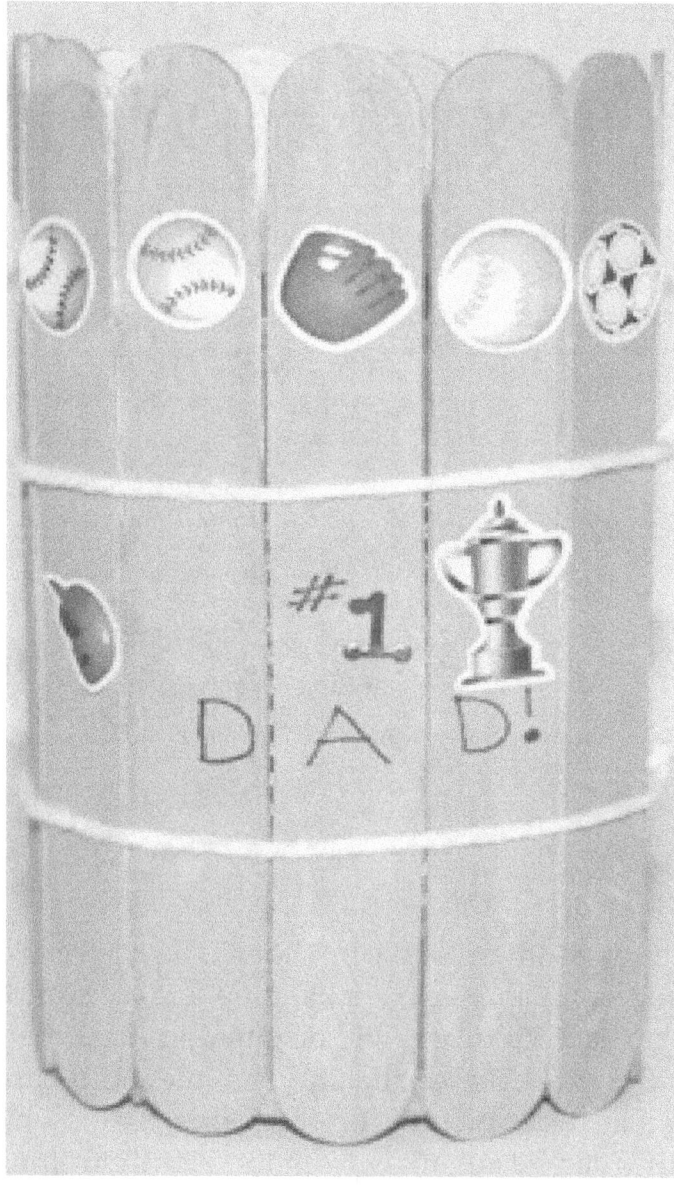

Need a place to store loose pencils? What is needed are an empty toilet paper holder, 15 Popsicle sticks, cardboard, paint or markers, tacky glue, rubber bands, and circles or star stickers. The first thing to do is to paint the Popsicle sticks and let them dry. Then trace the end of the toilet paper holder onto the cardboard. This will form a circle that will be cut out. Next, glue the circle onto one end of the cardboard tube. After that is dry, cover the tube lightly with tacky glue. Place the Popsicle sticks side-by-side to cover the tube. Wrap with the rubber bands until they are dry and then decorate with circles, stars, glitters or such other stickers.

A Butterfly Wand

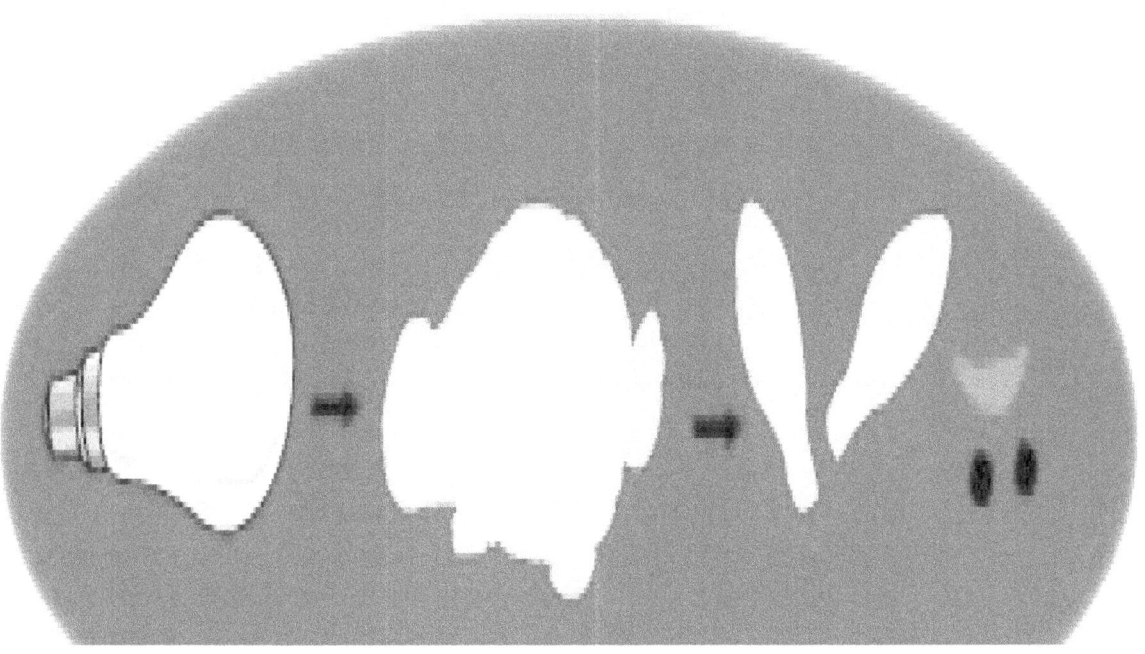

This is really great for parties. The materials needed are a Popsicle stick, a pipe cleaner, a cone-shaped coffee filter, crayons and glue (hot glue gun works best, but with an elder's assistance.) First glue the pipe cleaner to a Popsicle stick and make sure it cools completely. Then open up coffee filter at the seam. Decorate it with crayons. The last step is attaching the paper to the Popsicle stick with the pipe cleaner. Then bend the ends to form its antenna.

Sun Mask

Project 37

This is great for bright days. What is needed are a piece of heavy cardboard, a pencil, scissors, markers, masking tape and gold-coloured tinsel. First draw a large circle on the cardboard and cut the circle out. Draw about 8-10 triangles for the sun-rays and then cut them out. Next, draw where the eyes will go on the cardboard and cut out. Colour all of the pieces with the markers. Tape the triangles on to one side of the circle. Draw and cut out a rectangular piece of cardboard for the mask's handle, and tape it to the circle as well. Last but not the least, add some tinsel for extra shine.

SECTION 1

Craft Ideas from Nature

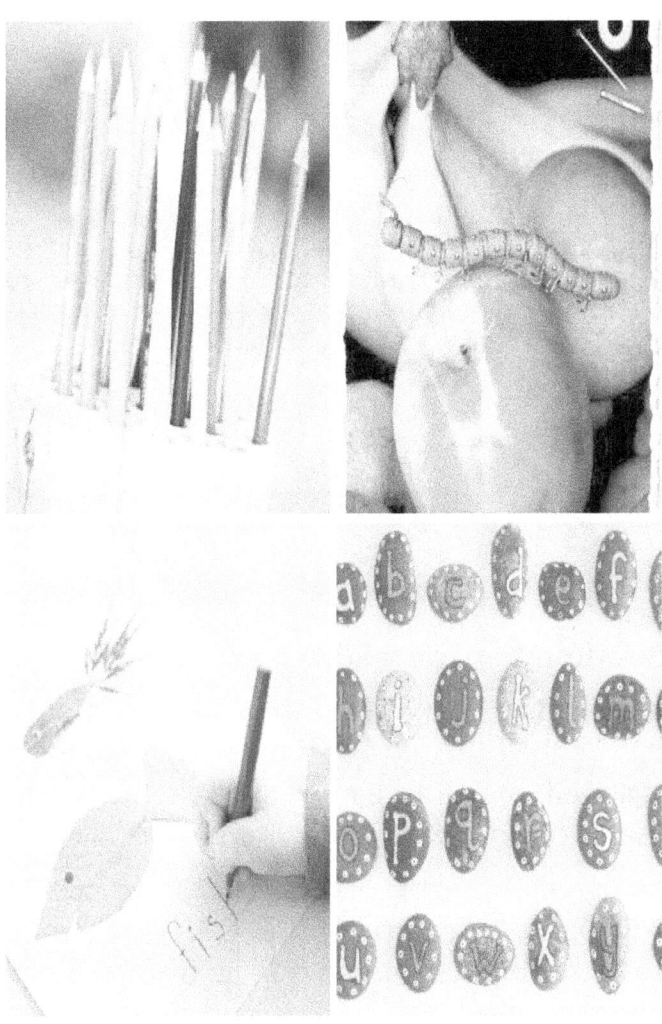

Making arts and crafts is a lot of fun, especially if you are able to do it with things from nature. The outside world is filled with so many natural things and the types of crafts that can be created with these elements of Nature are unlimited. Things, such as wreaths, jewellery and mirrors are just a few of the many examples. A good field trip outside to collect such interesting items of nature is a great activity for exercise, education and pleasure. Crafts created from scraps or other natural objects make excellent gifts. It almost feels like you're giving away a piece of the Earth, when you gift it to somebody!

Here are some craft ideas using items collected from the Mother Nature.

Seashell Wind Chime

Do your kids collect shells at the beach? How about making something crafty with those shells? Next time, you walk on the shore, grab as many shells as you possibly can. Shells are generally fragile, so it is best to have extras just in case a few break.

Next, get ready with your other supplies. Have some fishing wire, a head screwdriver, scissors and a curved branch or something similar, ready to go. Once these items are with you, wash out the shells and make sure that they are completely clean. After this task is completed, use the screwdriver to bore a hole in each shell. Children may ask the adults to perform this part.

Measure out some fishing line and cut it. Then thread it through the hole in to the shell and tie a knot to hold it. Tie the other end of the fishing wire to the curved branch. You can repeat this activity by adding more shells to the wire or by adding more wires of shells. That is up to your child's preference.

You can be as creative as you want to be by decorating the branch or by adding various shell shapes. In order to complete this craft, grab more fishing line, tie it to both ends of the branch, and hang it from a hook. **_Your beautifull Seashell Wind Chime is ready!_**

Scented Rocks

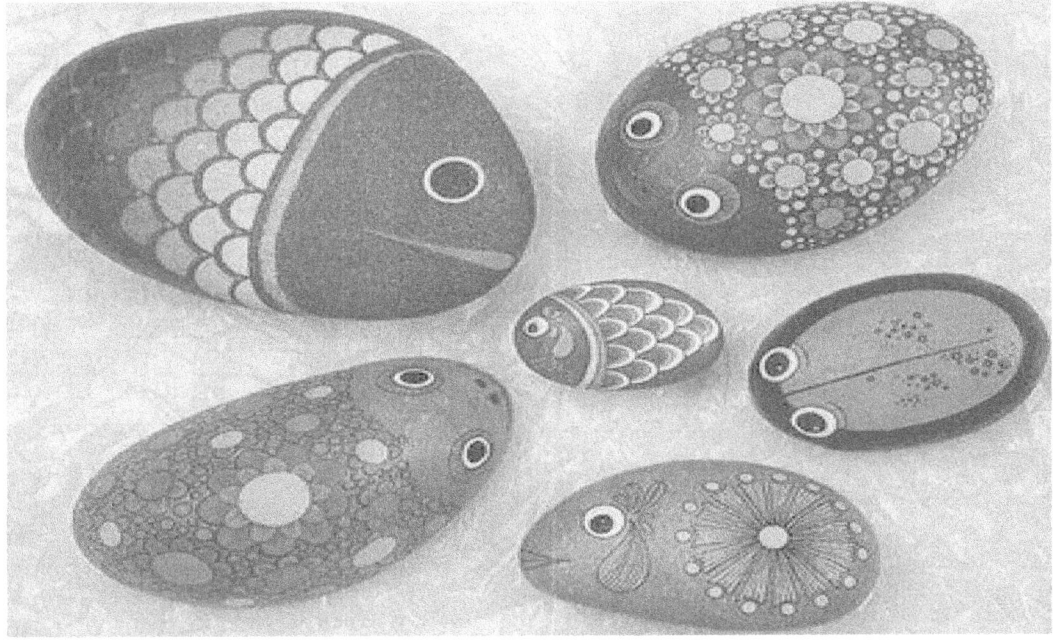

This activity creates very pretty craft items. Here's all that you need:
- ▲ ½ cup flour
- ▲ ½ cup salt
- ▲ teaspoon of essential oil
- ▲ 2/3 cup of boiling water
- ▲ Food colouring

First mix the flour and salt. Add the essential oil, followed by the boiling water. Add food colouring to the mix. When the mix has cooled down, shape the mix into balls about an inch in size. The dough will harden after a few days. Paint faces, flowers, or designs on the "rocks" for a personal touch. These *Scented Rocks* cna look very attractive in your drawing room or any other place as decorative items.

Rock Necklace

Project 40

This activity is fun and easy, particularly for kids who are fond of collecting rocks and bring home pockets full of special rocks. All you will need are one of those rocks, strips of some hemp, and a glue gun. Start by cutting a one yard piece of hemp. Using the glue gun, attach the hemp to the back of the rock. Wrap the hemp around the rock a few times and glue to make it secure. Lastly, tie the ends of the hemp together. *Your unique Rock Necklace is ready to wear!*

SECTION K

Craft Ideas for the Birds

Making crafts with your children can be a great fun and learning experience too! They involve a lot of creativity and patience. Crafts can be given away as gifts, or as decorations around the home. No matter what they are used for, they are definitely a way to have fun with your kids.

By using items from nature, children have the opportunity to explore and find things that are part of the great outdoors. It is cool to see what you can make out of sticks, rocks, leaves or seashells. Crafts that are prepared from nature can result in either very simple creations or very elaborate works of art.

What are some of the things that can be made from such natural materials? The following art and craft lessons will provide some suggestions for such crafty and natural creations! Go ahead to learn more...

Cheerios Bird Feeder

The birds will love this. Here are the items that you will need:
- Pencil
- Sugar ice cream cone
- Pipe cleaner
- Table knife
- Creamy peanut butter
- Cheerios
- Birdseed

Poke a hole in the pointed end of the ice cream cone with the pencil. Twist a knot in the end of the pipe cleaner and thread it into the ice cream cone and out the hole. Using the knife, spread the peanut butter onto the exterior of the cone. Press the Cheerios onto the peanut butter until the cone is completely covered. Next, sprinkle birdseed onto the cone, using your fingers to press it. *This looks lovely! The birds will indeed be in for a delicious treat.*

Project 42

Bird Binoculars

Children will get a kick out of this activity. The materials needed are:

- ▲ 2 paper rolls, about 4"- 5" long
- ▲ Single hole punch
- ▲ Glue
- ▲ Yarn or string

Ask your child to glue the two paper rolls together. Then poke holes in each side of the binoculars. Next, put the yarn or string through the holes and tie the ends together. Your child is now ready to go bird watching outside. This is a fun and easy natural activity! Isn't it?

SECTION L

Pipe Cleaner Crafts for Kids

Creating things out of pipe cleaners can be a really fun activity. The possibilities are endless. Kids can make dolls or animals with the help of different embellishments. For example, a cotton ball can be used for a doll's hair or sequins can be used for earrings.

The following list will describe how to create such cool things. Kids will be able to elaborate or decorate as freely as they want.

Kids Love Dinosaurs

Here is how to make a dinosaur out of pipe cleaners. What you need:
- Eight green pipe cleaners
- Googly eyes
- Pencil
- Marker
- Glue

Directions:
1. Connect three pipe cleaners from end to end.
2. Bundle them around a marker to create the body.
3. Connect two pipe cleaners from end to end.
4. Bundle half of it around a pencil to create the head and then coil some for the neck. Leave about a one-inch stem.
5. Insert the stem into the body in order to attach the head and neck. Coil one pipe cleaner around the pencil to create the tail.
6. Leave a one-inch attaching stem for the tail as well. By bending two cleaners into the shape of "V's", you can create the legs. Use the pencil for coiling.
7. Insert the legs into the body between the coils and then glue on the googly eyes. For more holding power, use the glue.

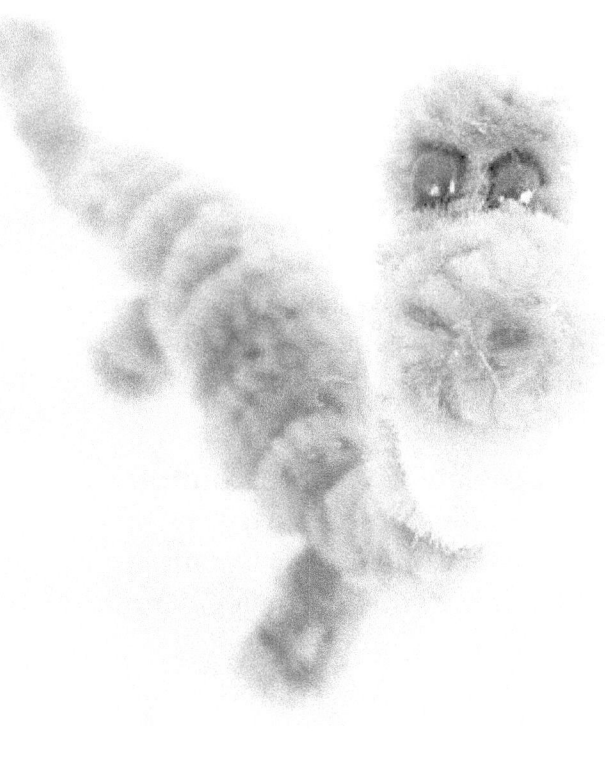

Don't let the dinosaur get lonely! In order to make a person along with the dinosaur, this is what you need:

- ▲ Four yellow pipe cleaners
- ▲ Googly eyes
- ▲ Pencil
- ▲ Fingernail clippers
- ▲ Glue

First make a "V" with a pipe cleaner and twist a small loop at the top. By twisting the two ends, you can create the person's torso.

Coil another pipe cleaner around a pencil and then slide it on to the torso.

With the fingernail clippers, clip another pipe cleaner in half and slide one half through the loop.

To create the head, bundle a pipe cleaner around a pencil and stick it on the loop. By making loops at the ends of the legs and arms, you can make the hands and feet.

Last, but not the least, glue on the googly eyes. With the extra pieces of pipe cleaner, you can make items, such as a tie or a suitcase for your little person.

Project 44

Hand Puppets are Fun for Everyone!

To make a hand puppet, here is what you'll need:
- Googly eyes
- One sock
- Cotton balls
- Fabric glue
- Felt
- Yarn
- Scissors
- Markers
- Pipe cleaners

Directions:
1. Start with a single, and clean sock. Make sure that the sock can fit comfortably over the child's hand.
2. Have the child work his or her thumb and fingers like a mouth.
3. With the marker, mark where the mouth, eyes, nose and ears would be.
4. Cut the ear and mouth shapes from the felt and glue where the marked areas are on the sock.
5. Glue the googly eyes on to the sock and use the cut up pieces of yarn for the hair.
6. Finish with the pipe cleaners to create horns or antennas.

SECTION M

Create Crafts from Nature

Crafts can be made from almost anything. If your child likes the outdoors, why not discover the different types of things that could be used for craft activities? From flowers to rocks, and everything in between, crafts from nature are very cool.

Next time you are outside with your child, whether it is for exercise, a jaunt to the mailbox, or for a breath of fresh air, gather some items that you think could be made into cool crafts.

The following chapters offer of a few suggestions for some craft ideas made by nature.

Project 45

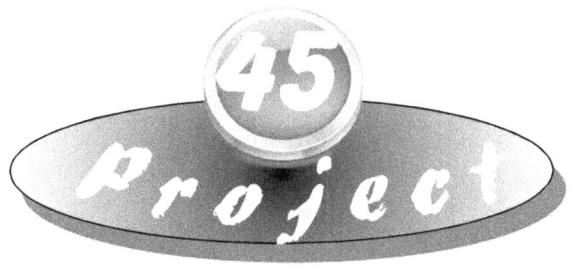

Nature Bracelet

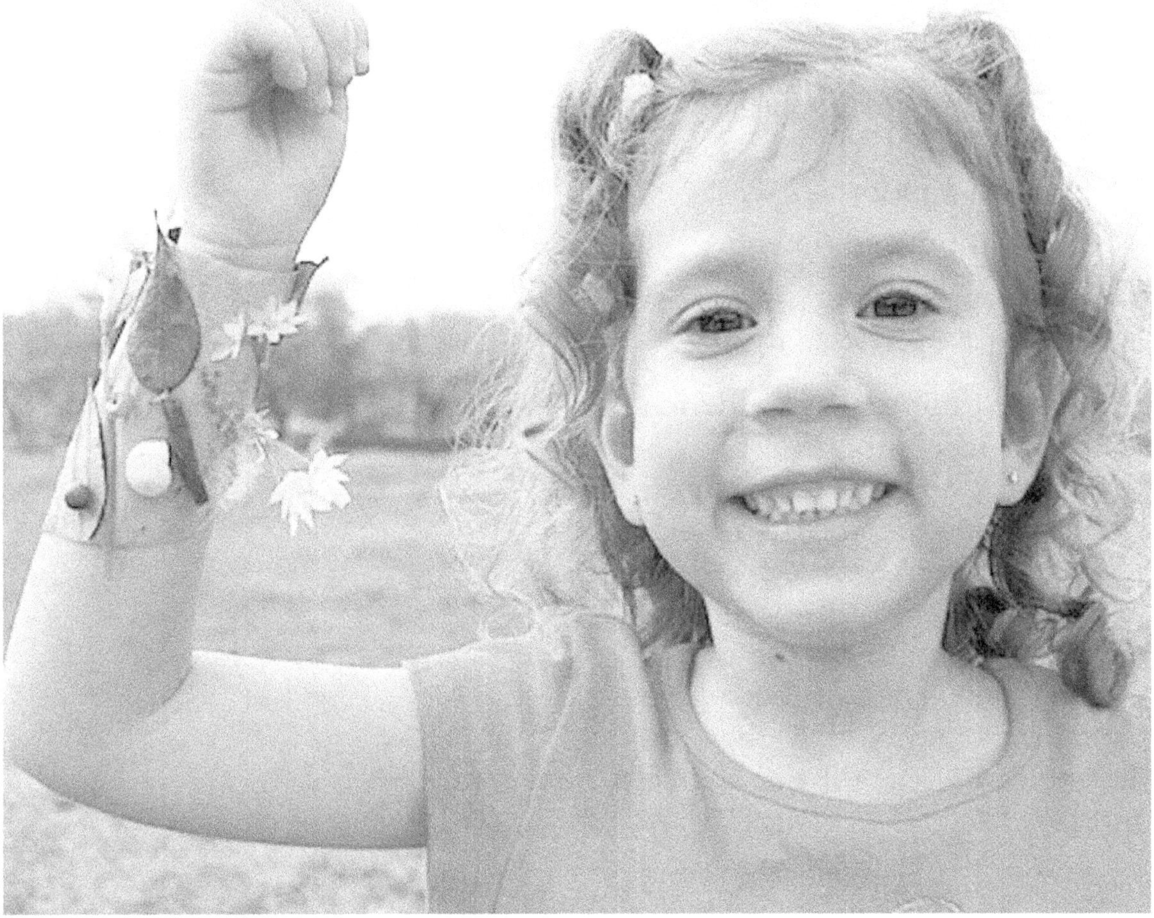

This activity is very easy. It can be as colourful as your child wants it to be. All you need to begin with is a masking tape. Tear off some masking tape and wrap it around your child's wrist. Make sure that the sticky side is on the outside. To decorate it, go outside and find items that your child would like for the bracelet. It can be decorated with pretty flowers, small twigs or blades of grass.

Switch Plate of Flowers

This will add something pleasant to any room. Here are all the materials needed:

- Clear plastic switch plate
- White craft glue
- Small paintbrush
- Small pressed flowers
- Coloured paper
- Utility knife

It is best to purchase a switch plate that has both a front cover and a back cover. Use coloured paper to put into the switch plate. The paper will be used as the background. An adult should use the utility knife to cut the paper. Use the back cover of the switch plate as a size guide. Make sure that holes are cut for the switch and small screws as well.

Now it is time to add the flowers. With the paintbrush, get some glue and place some glue on the flowers to put onto the coloured paper. Remember to note where the switch and the screws will actually go later.

Once all of the flowers are glued, set it down to dry for a little while. Now, your masterpiece is completely dry. Place the decorated paper between the front and back covers of the switch plate. The final step is to attach it to the wall.

Wow! This looks amazing.

Driftwood Door Handle

Have you ever thought of adding some style to something by using driftwood? This activity will bring out the carpenter in you. Here are the materials needed:

- A unique piece of driftwood
- Pencil
- Tape measure
- Two sturdy screws
- An electric drill or super glue
- A wooden door

Clean up the driftwood so that it's rid of dirt or debris. Position the driftwood on the door as you would like it. If there is already a handle on the door, remove it. Have your child hold the driftwood up against the door. Using the tape measure, measure where the screws will go with your pencil on the front and back of the door. Adults, use the electric drill to screw the next handle on or use super glue instead. Enjoy!

Festive Bow and Arrow

Project 48

Any play on Ramayana is incomplete without the bow and arrow *(Teer Kamaan)*. You can make your own bow and arrow, too, but be careful not to hurt anyone.

You will need:
- Elastic or strong cord
- Broomstick
- Plasticine
- Stem of any tree
- Scissors
- Paints

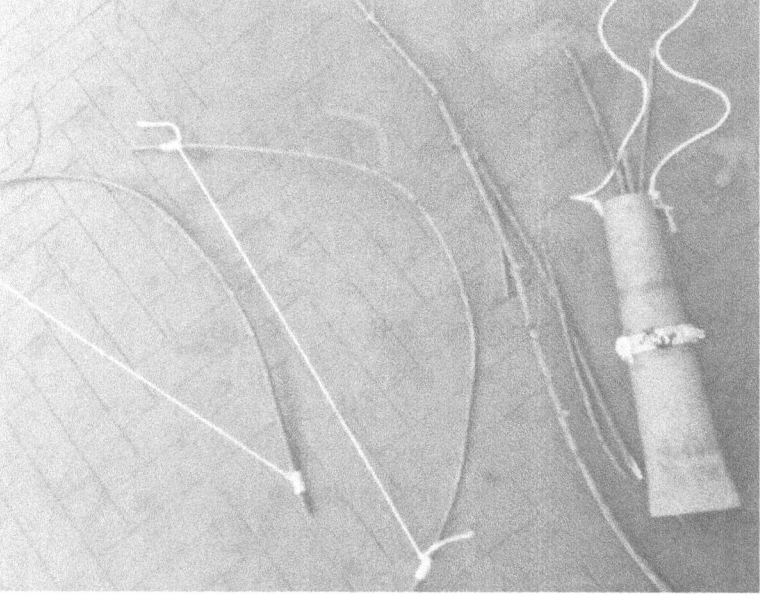

Bend the stem in the form of an arc making sure it does not break. Tie an elastic from one end to the other.

For the arrow, take one stick out from the broom. Trim it.

Make a ball out of the plasticine and stick it at one end of the arrow. This will not hurt anyone while you play with your bow and arrow. Easy, yet classy! Isn't it?

Project 49
Make a Card of Webbed Veins

The leaves of the Peepal tree have a beautiful shape - they taper to a needle-point. And when these green leaves brush against each other, they constantly make a rustling sound that attracts everyone's attention.

Even when the leaves dry, leaving behind a webbed skeleton of veins, they look grand, i.e., grand enough to be made into *greeting cards*.

The things you need:
- ▲ Peepal leaves
- ▲ Black chart paper
- ▲ Scissors
- ▲ Adhesive

Soak the Peepal leaf in water for seven to eight hours.

Take it out and wash it under a stream of running water. Dry and paste it on the top of a card.

Send out these handmade cards to all your friends. *They will really love and admire your art and craft skills!*

Eco-friendly Holi Colours

Project 50

There was a time when the colours that were used by people to play Holi were taken from nature – i.e., from flowers, leaves, etc. Why not revive those memories again? Use natural colours of the nature to paint the town red!

The things you need:

- Tesu flowers: Half a kilogram
- Strainer

Dried tesu flowers are readily available in the market. You can look for them in grocery stores or shops that sell Holi colours, or in the old city areas.

Boil half a bucket of water and soak the tesu flowers in it overnight.

Strain the mixture to get a yellowish orange liquid and get ready to splash on the Holi Fastival.

This natural colour does not have any side effects on the skin.

Have a happy and safe Holi!

SECTION N

Better than Diamonds: Macaroni Jewellery!

Macaroni crafts are great activities for children. On a rainy day or during "down time," kids can work on a number of different projects. Making jewelry out of macaroni can be a really fun activity for kids and their parents. Although it may seem like a silly thing to do, it is actually quite simple. Just go to your pantry and find a box of macaroni and cheese. Save the cheese packet for an extra cheesy meal later and get creative with the pasta or the macaroni!

A Necklace for Every Occasion

Project 51

Macaroni bead necklaces can be given to friends or relatives as a cute little gift. Here is how to make one in some very easy steps. Before starting, make sure you have the macaroni, plus the following items:

- Tape
- Food Colouring
- String
- Scissors
- Rubbing alcohol
- Measuring cups
- Spoon

If your child would like the macaroni coloured, do the food colouring first by mixing food colouring and rubbing alcohol. The best type for this activity is liquid food colouring.

Pour cup of rubbing alcohol into a 12 to 16 oz cup and add anywhere from five to 15 drops of colour.

To create even more colours, have your child mix two different colours together for more variety.

Next add the macaroni into the cup. Stir until all the colour is absorbed.

Spoon the macaroni onto a paper towel and let it dry.

Once the macaroni is dry, the jewellery making is ready to begin.

After the colouring task is the completed, determine how long your child wants the necklace by cutting the string at the desired length. Wrap one end of the string with a tape so that sliding macaroni on to the string will be a little easier.

Slide a piece of macaroni all the way to the end of the string and tie a knot around it. This will help prevent the other macaroni from sliding off from the end.

Continue to add macaroni until the string is full.

Tie each end of the string together to complete the necklace. With the different coloured macaroni, a child can get creative with various colour patterns. ***Your colourful, glamorous Macaroni Necklace is ready to wear!***

Bracelets Made Easy

Project 52

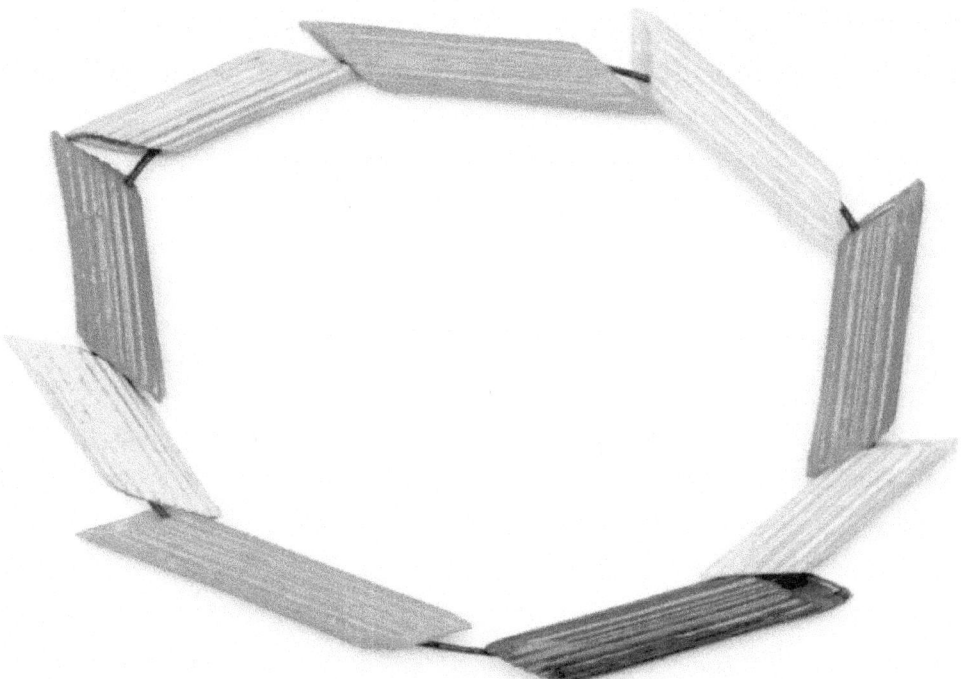

Creating bracelets can be fun as well by following the same simple instructions. Your child can be creative by using as many colours as he or she desires by using colourful macaroni pieces. There are several sizes of macaroni as well, and that means more variety. Mix and match the macaroni.

Depending upon the occasion, a child can mix colours that work well with various seasons. For example, you can string red and green coloured macaroni together for Christmas presents or string together orange and black coloured macaroni together for Diwali festivities.

Also, if your child would like to eat the necklaces created, using Cheerios instead of Macaroni can be used as a substitute. No matter the preference, this is a fun activity for children and it allows them to get as creative as they want to be.

SECTION 0

Craft Ideas Using Recycled Materials

Making craft items out of recycled materials is a great way to *reuse and recycle*. These activities should not be limited to just aluminium cans and plastic bottles. Things, such as old shoe boxes can be recycled and reused as well.

It is harmful for our planet, Earth to waste so many reusable materials. The next time your child has any free time, look around your house and yard and collect some materials. Instead of dumping things in the trash, reuse them and make them last forever.

Candleholder

Project 53

This is a great gift idea for birthdays and holidays. After making food in the kitchen, save some cans for your children. They can be turned into beautiful candleholders instead of piling up in the trash or the dustbin.

A small 5 oz. can will work best. The other materials needed are some clip art, rubber bands, hammer, nails and spray paint. To make your can nice and smooth, first wash out any leftover sauce and fill it with water. Put it in the freezer. Take the help of your computer and help your child pick up some cool clip art and print those out.

Cover the can with the clip art and secure with a rubber band. Take the help of an adult to poke holes in the can shaping the clip art with the hammer and nail. Then let the ice melt, have it dry and spray paint on it. The last step is to add a tea light candle. *Now this is really brilliant! Isn't it?*

54

project

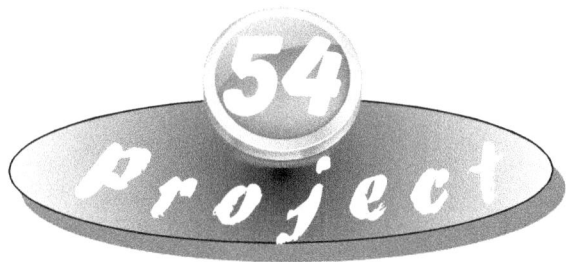

Soda Can Pen Holder

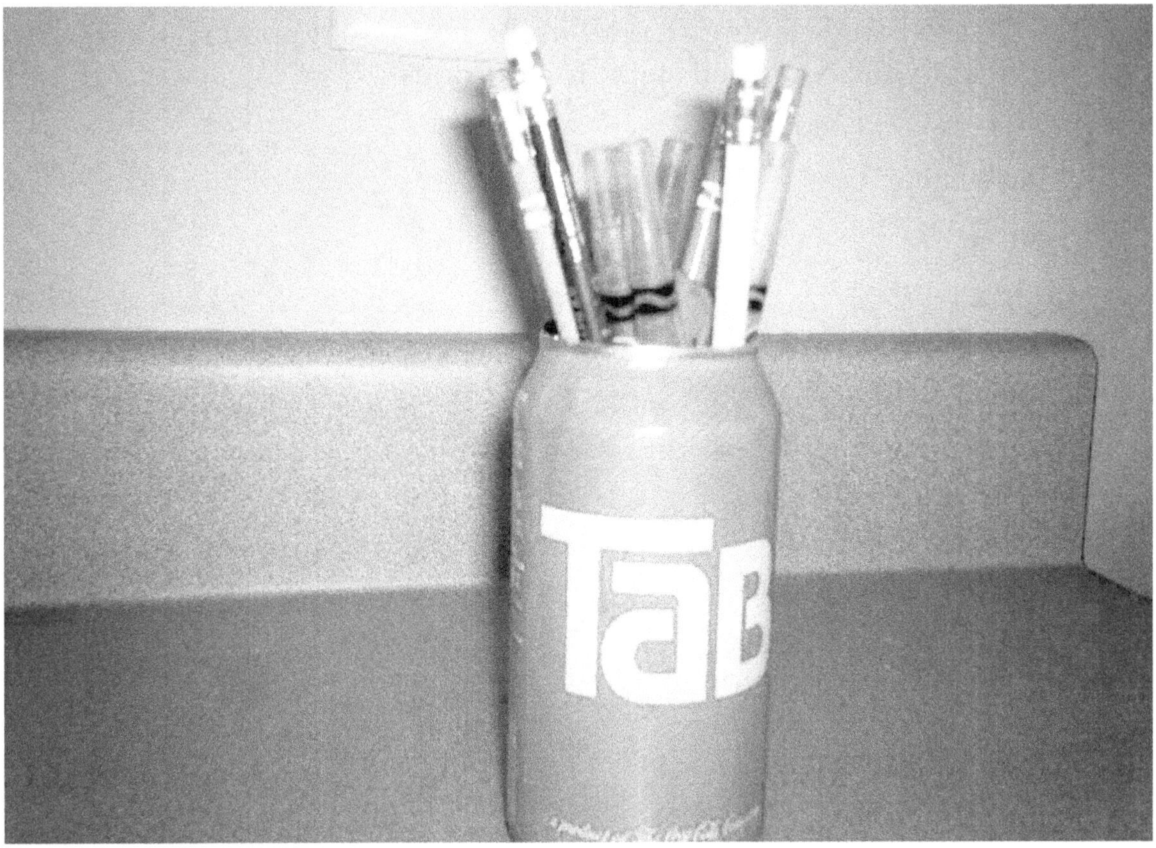

Save one or two of your favourite soda cans before recycling. Make your office supplies stand out with this fun and easy activity. The only other thing that you will need is a can opener. Just take off the top by using the can opener and find some pens to put in. To weigh the can down, throw some washers to the bottom.

Pencil Stand of Bangles

Project 55

If you have old bangles lying around in the house that nobody wears, you can use them to make a pencil stand for your desk.

The things you need:
- Old bangles
- Adhesive
- Cardboard
- Scissors
- Pencil

Collect bangles of different colours but of the same size.

Use a bangle to draw a circle on the cardboard piece. Cut it.

Now stick one bangle on top of the other using the circular cardboard as the base for your pencil stand.

Stick the bangles till you get a height of four inches. That is it. There is no need to paint or decorate. It will be the most colourful pencil stand that you have ever had!

A Bunny Rabbit

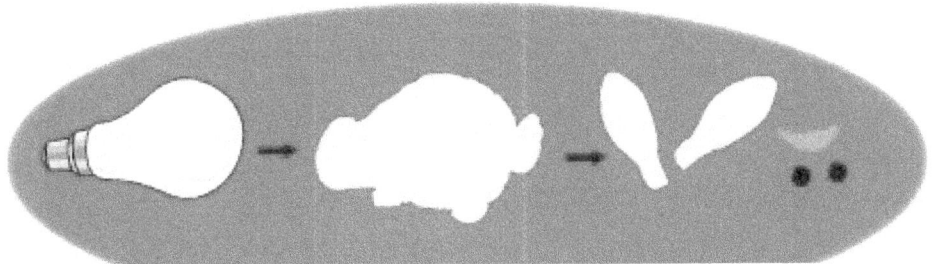

If you wish to make a toy at home that does not take much time, then try this. It looks cute and can be added to your soft toy collection.

The things you need:
- Fused bulb
- Cotton
- Adhesive
- Black pepper corns
- Velvet paper or the Indian 'Bindi'
- Scissors

Take a bulb and stick cotton on it, covering it completely. Give additional padding of cotton for the mouth of the rabbit.

Cut out the cotton in the shape of rabbit ears and stick them to the rabbit's head.

Also, stick four cotton balls for the legs and one for the tail.

Finally, stick two black pepper corns for the eyes and cut the velvet paper or 'bindi' in a crescent shape to make the mouth.

And, if you wish to make whiskers, then you can use a plastic string, or finer hair of the broomstick.

Can-Do Robots

Project 57

These friendly robots are more than just good-looking; magnets hold their features in place, making the robots, the metallic equivalent of a Mr. Potato Head.

What you'll need:
- A tin can
- Electrical tape (optional)
- Hardware and various other recyclables, such as bottle caps, keys, etc.
- Hot-glue gun
- Strong disk magnets

Open a tin can with a safety can opener so that there are no sharp edges. (If you only have a regular opener, line the inside of the can's rim with electrical tape.)

Empty, wash and then dry the can.

For facial features, arms, propulsion devices and communication arrays, look for items around the house and at the hardware store. You can use bolts, brackets, hinges, keys, switches, bottle caps, washers, knobs, and many such objects.

Hot-glue the items to strong disk magnets. This step is optional.

You can just fix and fit the items collected to complete your *toy robots* and get ready to play!

SECTION P

Recycle, Reduce and Reuse: Arts and Crafts

Crafts can be made out of anything. They can be given away as gifts or kept at home. Doing craft activities with children will engage them in following directions as well as being proud of something that they made themselves.

Because crafts can vary, why not something make out of recycled materials? Items, such as aluminium cans, plastic bottles or old coffee tins can be transformed into so many different and interesting things.

Soda Tab Jewellery

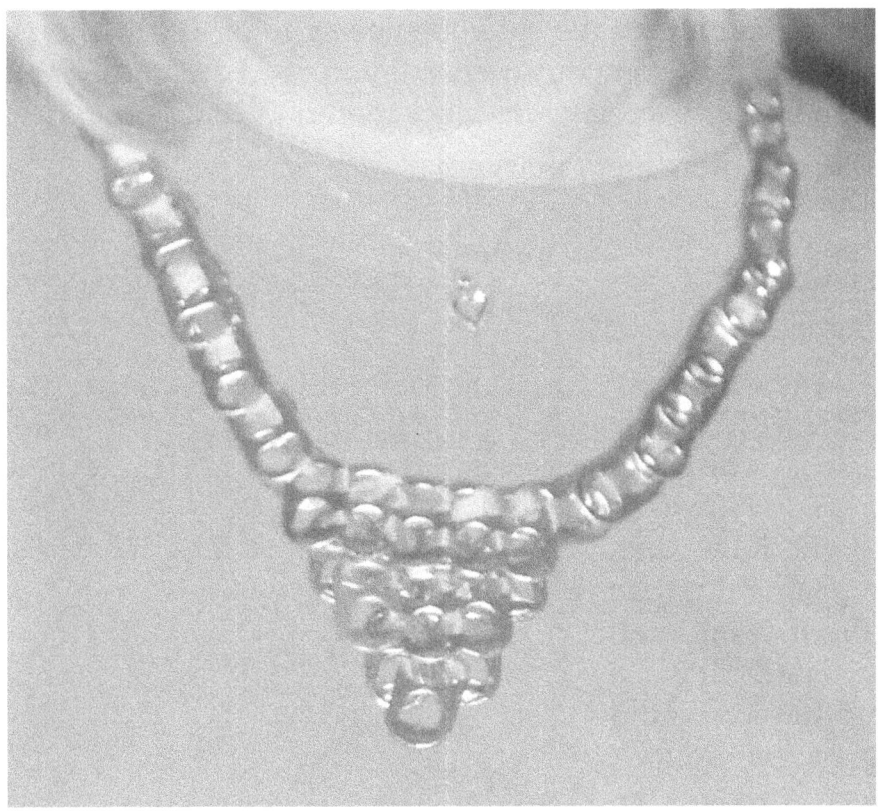

Keep the tabs off the soda cans and become a *jewellery designer*. Have your child remove the tabs from different soda cans. See how many he or she can collect. The other materials needed are jump rings, washers, jewellery wire, and jewellery cutting tools.

Cut the thick, middle part out of the tabs and using the jewellery tool, open the jump rings. Slip the soda tab through and close the jump ring. Add as many tabs as you want to make a really long and dazzling necklace.

Bottle Cap Magnets

You can buy magnets at the convenience store or at gift shops. However, they are easy to make on your own. All you need are bottle caps from your empty soda bottles. Here are the other materials that you may require:

- Coloured permanent markers
- Glue
- Felt
- Magnet

This project will look best with bottle caps of different colours. However, if you don't have that, you can elaborate with stickers or other coloured markers. First, draw a design of what you would like your magnet to look like. Then arrange the bottle caps. Glue them together so that they will stay in place.

Using the coloured permanent markers, draw on the bottle caps by adding eyes or whatever you wish. Place your marker on a piece of felt and trace around the shape onto the felt. Cut the pattern out along the traced line. Glue the newly shaped felt piece to the bottle cap shape. Once the glue is dry, glue the magnet to the back of the felt. Place it on the fridge and admire your art!

Project 60: Faux Leather Pencil Holder

This craft makes a great gift for dads. Here is what you need to get started:

- ▲ Empty can
- ▲ Masking tape
- ▲ Brown shoe polish
- ▲ Old rag
- ▲ ½ sheet of brown felt
- ▲ Scissors
- ▲ Brown or Earth tone beads
- ▲ Hot glue gun
- ▲ Acrylic sealer spray

Be sure the empty can is washed inside and out and completely dry. Trace a circle from the can on to the brown felt and set the felt aside.

Tear off pieces of masking tape and cover the can completely with it, including the bottom and overlapping the rim.

Apply brown shoe polish all over the masking tape. The more you use the darker it will get. Wipe off the excess with an old rag. Set aside to dry completely.

Cut around the circle shape on the felt (see Step 1) NOT on the lines, but about ½" around the outside and inside of the line you traced. This will make a ring.

Using the line you traced as your guide, pipe a line of hot glue on to the felt. Quickly place the rim of the can on to the glue, adhering the felt ring to the top of the can.

With an adult's help, hot glue the sides of the felt down to the inside and outside of the can rim. Glue beads around the bottom edge of the brown felt on the outside of the can. Pull off any leftover hot glue strings to clean up your project. Spray can with acrylic sealer spray.

Tips:

Use good quality shoe polish, not the cheap kind. Cheap shoe polish is very watery and does not stain well.

For younger kids, you can skip the steps for the felt rim and use a line of masking tape instead. Have them string the beads onto a sturdy piece of yarn or cord and hot glue that around the rim for them.

Be sure to write "Father's Day" and the year you made it on the bottom of the can! A great piece of Craft indeed!

Project 61 — Painting Pots

We cannot paint the walls of our house, but we can definitely paint the pots in our house.

All you need is:

- ▲ Poster paints
- ▲ Paintbrush

Pick up a pot and remove any dust from it using a soft cloth or a brush.

If you have earthern pots, give them a coating of colour that you think would match with the colour of your walls.

Let this base colour dry. Now you can paint a variety of patterns on top to decorate your pots.

If your pots are cemented and polished, you can directly make patterns on them. It's quite interesting and at the same time colourful and attractive too!

Coffee Time

Project 62

Buy a few plain coffee mugs from the market or use the old ones and paint special designs for each member of your family or friends. They will love it.

The things you need:
- Oil or acrylic colours
- Paint brushes
- Plain ceramic coffee mugs
- Turpentine oil

Wash the mugs with hot water and soap. Dry them and ensure that there are no grease or dirt stains.

Paint small motifs or write out a message for the person you are going to give the mug to. For instance, you can make a caricature or write any message that you may want: "for my lovely sister", "for you, Grandpa", or even a birthday message.

Painting Tip:

Wait for the first colour coat to dry before putting another.

Let the paint dry overnight.

In case, you feel that you can do much better, take a clean rag, dip it in turpentine oil and rub out whatever you have painted and start again. It's that simple, yet a great work of Art! Isn't it?

SECTION Q

Go Green with Your Craft Ideas

Saving the environment is a very important thing, especially when you can make cool crafts out of *recycled materials*. Almost anything can be recycled and children will love being involved in such a great activity. Before setting the garbage and recycling bins out every week, take a second to save a couple of items for arts and crafts.

Children can have fun and at the same time, it can be a good craft activity!

Gift Bag Recycling

Reuse gift bags that you have received by transforming them into something completely different. What you need is simply an old gift bag. A brown paper bag will also work as well. With handmade paper, glue, a pencil and a pair of scissors, your child can make something really interesting!

Carefully unglue the bottom flaps at the bottom of the old gift bag. Place the opened bag onto paper and draw the outlines slightly longer than the bag. Cut the paper, leaving some extra room that is enough to cover the bag. Apply glue to the old bag. Make sure that the glue is applied to the folds.

Place the handmade paper or silver or golden gift-wrap paper on the bag and align the bottom edges. Attach it to one side of the bag. Cut slits at the corners of the extra hanging handmade paper at the top of the bag. This will allow you to fold the extra paper down into the old bag. Make sure that you fold it down smoothly.

Now glue the bottom flaps. You can then decorate it with ribbons, glitters, stars, buttons, etc.

Kitty Condo

This is a great activity for using recycling materials and entertaining your cat. Here is what you will need:

- Two or more paper bags
- Scissors
- Glue
- Tape
- Cardboard
- Construction paper
- Glasses or bowls
- Pencil
- Loose pictures
- Your cat!

Lay the paper bags flat and using the bowls, trace a circle on the bottom of them. Then open the bags and cut out the circles. On the sides of the bags, trace circles by using the glasses. Cut these circles out too.

Cut some strips of cardboard and lay them inside of the bags for support. Place two of the bags top to top, and fit one of the bags inside the other about an inch. Glue or tape them in place. Continue these steps with the other bags. Decorate the outside of the bags by using the pictures or anything that you find fancy. To add extra support to the cat condo, glue some construction paper around the windows. Your Kitty Condo is ready for your Pussy Cat!

Handprint Paper Flowers

Project 65

A lovely bouquet of Handprint Paper Flowers are fun paper crafts for kids who love to express their creative prowess. Little ones can give these as gifts to their moms and dads on a special day. These handy, heartfelt crafts also make exciting school crafts.

What you need are as follows:

- Different colours of construction paper
- A child's hand
- Pen
- Scissors
- Glue
- Pipe cleaners

Trace your child's hand and then cut it out. Glue the bottom corners together leaving a little hole in the bottom to slide the pipe cleaners through. Tie a knot on one end of the pipe cleaner so that it won't slide out. After the flower is dry, stick the pipe cleaner through the hand, and bend the fingers back to give the flower a little flare. Now wasn't that easy and creative too?

Project 66: Make Your Own Musical Group

Create joyful noises with common household items with a little creativity. The instruments are grouped by type, such as: percussion, wind and string.

This is just a starter list. Add other kinds of instruments for different sound textures.

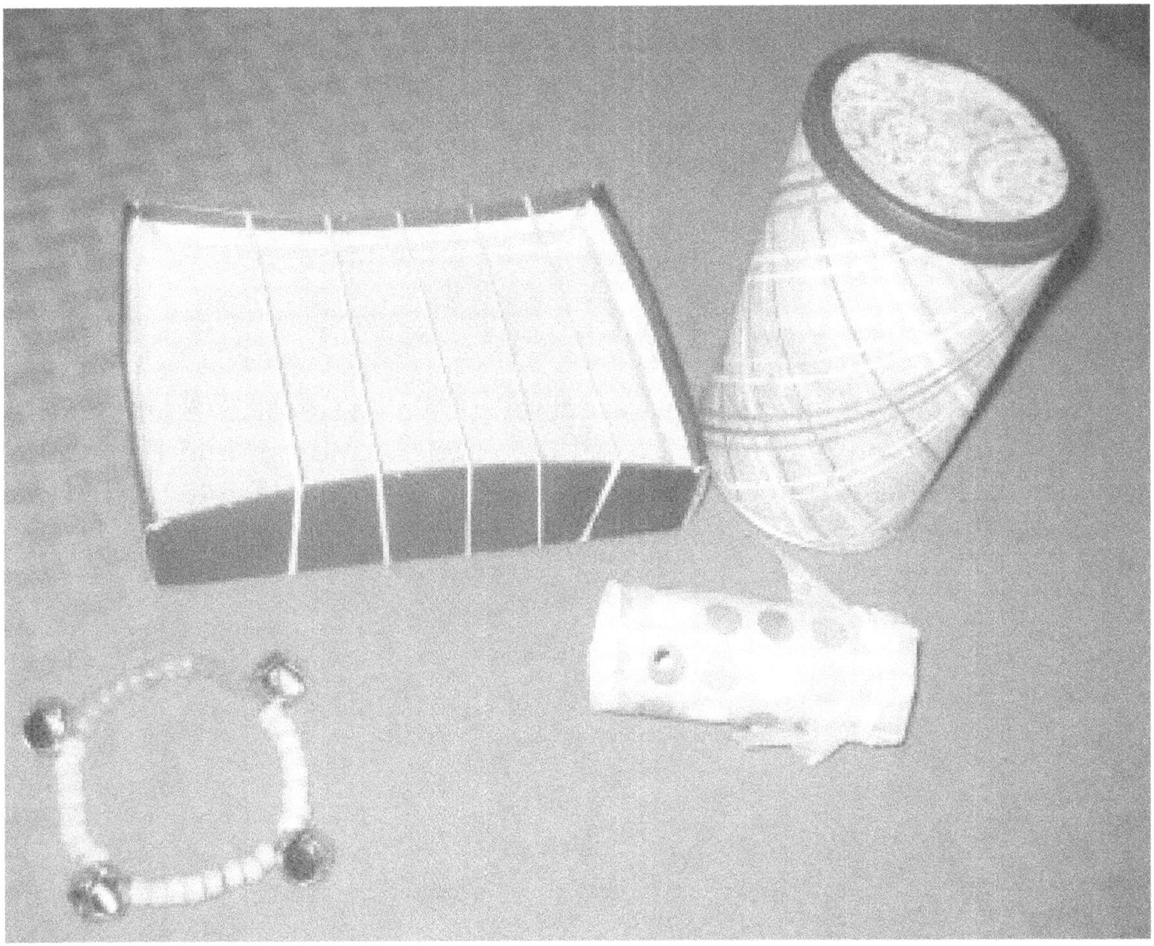

Percussion

- ▲ **Cymbals** – Use two pot lids
- ▲ **Drum** – Use a large pot or an upside down 5-gallon bucket with mixing spoons. For the best sound, raise the pot or bucket up on some sturdy blocks so that the sides can vibrate more freely.
- ▲ **Drinking glass xylophone** – Line up all the tall drinking glasses with different quantities of water in them. Arrange them in an ascending or descending order of pitch. Carefully strike with a spoon to make melodies.

Wind

- ▲ **Kazoo** – Take an empty toilet paper tube and a 4"x4" square of wax paper. Put the wax paper over one end of the tube and secure with the rubber band. Hum your favourite tune into the open end with your mouth against the cardboard. Another version – Fold the 4"x4" wax paper square over the teeth of a comb and put your lips against the comb and hum.
- ▲ **Voices** – Everyone has this instrument with them!

String

- ▲ **Rubberband Guitar** – Stretch several rubber bands of different widths around an empty shoe box. All the rubber bands should be parallel to each other. Attach a ruler or other flat stick to attach to the back of the shoe box. This is the neck (long part with the frets) of the guitar.

Paper Sack Costume

What you'll need:
- Paper grocery sack
- Scissors
- Four feet of yarn or string, cut into one-foot lengths
- Crayons, markers and other decorative items
- Glue or an adhesive

Take a paper grocery sack and cut out a hole in the bottom, large enough for a child's head to go through.

Turn the sack with that hole facing up, as if the child would be wearing it. Make another cut in the middle of the sack, right down the "back" of the costume.

Cut two arm holes in the sides of the sack, right where the side of the sack meets the bottom part. Do not cut into the bottom, just the sides. When the costume is on, the bottom of the sack will rest on the child's shoulders. The arm holes should be where the arms would naturally come out.

With a paper punch, put a hole on either side of the back of the neck of the costume. Tie and knot a length of string or yarn to each hole, leaving one end as long as possible to tie the costume on. Put another pair of paper punch holes about halfway down the back, repeating the step for tying the string.

Decorate the costume however the child wishes. When all the decoration is finished, allow the glue to dry (if any is used).

Add or create a mask to make your costume complete. If your child doesn't like masks, use hats, jewellery, or FDA-approved face paints instead.

Working on these pre-school crafts with your child will promote both their imagination and eye-hand coordination.

SECTION K

Arts and Crafts for Kids

Have you ever wondered what to do with your large empty plastic bottles? Now you can give them a second life as a craft project. Arts and crafts for kids can be more than just a fun way to pass the time. Use these projects to teach your kids about recycling and about our wonderful planet, the Earth.

Wave Maker

Project 68

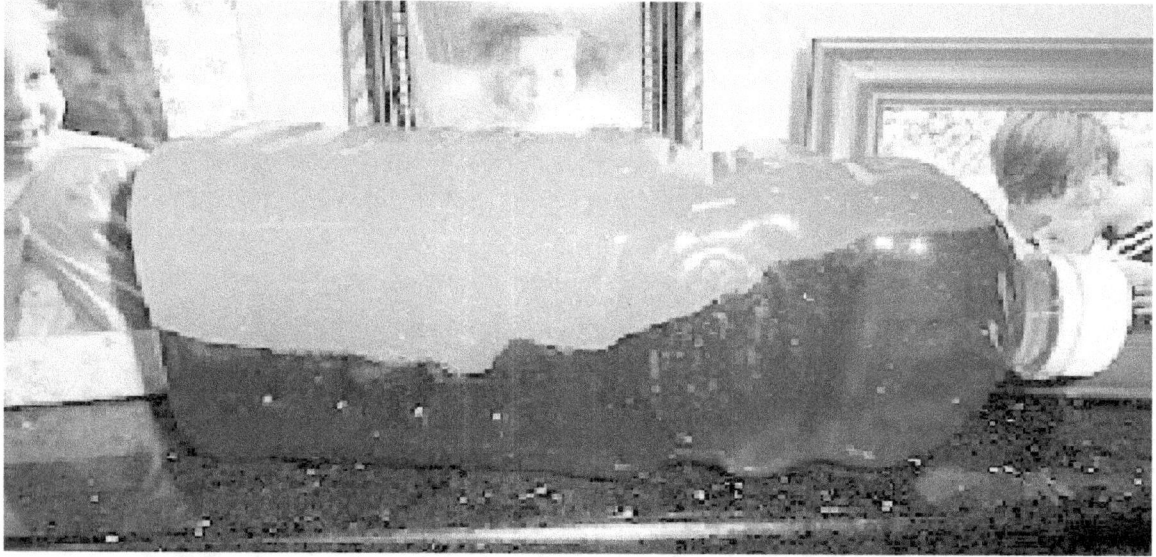

Mouthwash bottle, 2-litre soda bottle, large clear water bottle (the larger the better)

- Colourless vegetable oil
- Water
- Blue and green food colouring
- Packing tape or glue

Soak the bottle in a warm soapy water to remove the label. Fill the bottle halfway with the vegetable oil. Fill the remainder of the bottle with water until there is just a small air bubble left at the top. Add four or five drops of food colouring until you get the shade you like (as the ocean). Put the lid on as tight as you can, and tape or glue it. Shut it to keep it from leaking. Shake it up to see thousands of little bubbles, or sway it gently from side to side to see the rolling waves.

What a beautiful way to experience the ocean in a bottle!

Project 69: Treasure Bottle

Mouthwash bottle, a 2-litre-soda bottle, large clear water bottle (the larger the better)

Several cups of uncooked rice (depends on your bottle)

Small treasure items – trinkets, tiny dollar-store plastic toys, buttons, beads, coins, charms, plastic bugs or spiders, plastic rings, small pebbles, pieces of hard candy, etc.

Procedure

Soak the bottle in a warm soapy water to remove the label. Fill the bottle two-third with uncooked rice. Add the small trinkets and other treasure items. Screw the cap on tightly. Turn and roll the bottle over to mix the small items in with the rice. Watch as the treasures appear and disappear and as the rice moves in the bottle. Take note that the larger and heavier items (coins, heavy beads, etc.) will stay more centred in the bottle, and the lighter items will stay around the edges, and be more visible.

Soda Bottle Bird Feeder

- Plastic bottle
- Two wooden spoons
- Sharpie marker
- Craft knife
- Scissors
- Floral wire

With a sharpie marker, draw a small circle on one side of the bottle about 4 inches from the bottom. Cut it out (using a craft knife) and make sure that the end of the spoon fits snugly into the hole.

Directly opposite this hole, cut a slightly larger hole (using a craft knife and scissors). Make sure the big end of the spoon can rest in the hole.

Repeat this process approximately 2 inches from the bottom of the soda bottle, but use the opposite sides of the bottle so that your spoons are at a 90 degree angle to one another.

Fill the bottle with birdseeds. Make sure to do this in an area where you can sweep up the mess!

Make a hanger out of the floral wire and secure to the top of the bottle. Screw the top on and hang from your favourite place.

Remarkable and unique, isn't it?.

Kazoo

You can make a kazoo out of a toilet paper tube. It is an easy and fun activity for kids. All you need is an empty tube, black paint, foam brush, foam music notes, tacky glue, wax paper, a rubber band and scissors.

First paint the tube with the black tube. After it is dry, glue on the music notes. Cut a 6" circle out of the wax paper and secure it with the rubber band at one end of the tube. Create your own kind of music by tooting through the open end of the tube. Have fun!

QUIZ BOOKS

ENGLISH IMPROVEMENT

OTHERS LANGUAGE

ACTIVITIES BOOK

QUOTES/SAYINGS

BIOGRAPHIES/CHILDREN SCIENCE LIBRARY

Set Code: 02122 S

COMPUTER BOOKS

All books available at **www.vspublishers.com**

STUDENT DEVELOPMENT/LEARNING

POPULAR SCIENCE

PUZZLES

DRAWING BOOKS

VALUE PACKS

COMPREHENSIVE COMPUTER LEARNING	SECURE A JOB	QUIZ TIME	सम्पूर्ण आत्म-विकास	महिलोपयोगी	छात्रोपयोगी	मनोरंजन का खज़ाना
(12410S)	(00608S)	(02312S)	(00223S)	(14001S)	(10505S)	(12211S)

Contact us at sales@vspublishers.com

HINDI LITERATURE

TALES & STORIES

All Books Fully Coloured

MUSIC (संगीत)

MAGIC & FACT (जादू एवं तथ्य)

ACADEMIC BOOKS

MYSTERIES (रहस्य)

All books available at www.vspublishers.com

CAREER & BUSINESS MANAGEMENT

CONCISE DICTIONARIES

 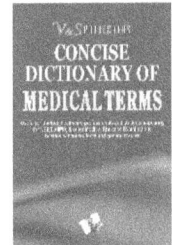

  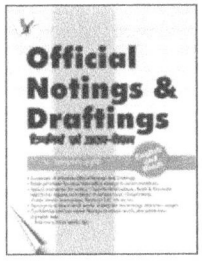 

Contact us at sales@vspublishers.com

www.ingramcontent.com/pod-product-compliance
Lightning Source LLC
Chambersburg PA
CBHW080553230426
43663CB00015B/2823